The Art
— of —
Translating Prose

Burton Raffel

The Pennsylvania State University Press
University Park, Pennsylvania

Chapter 6 appeared in slightly different form under the title "Translating Cervantes:
Una Vez Mas" in *Cervantes* 13, no. 1 (Spring 1993): 5-30.

Library of Congress Cataloging-in-Publication Data

Raffel, Burton.
    The art of translating prose / Burton Raffel.

        p.   cm.
    Includes bibliographical references and index.
    ISBN 0-271-01080-0
    1. Translating and interpreting.   I. Title
PN241.R28   1994
                        418'.02—dc20   93-20439
                                                   CIP

Published by The Pennsylvania State University Press,
Barbara Building, Suite C, University Park, PA 16802-1003

It is the policy of The Pennsylvania State University Press to use acid-free paper for
the first printing of all clothbound books. Publications on uncoated stock satisfy
the minimum requirements of American National Standard for Information
Sciences—Permanence of Paper for Printed Library Materials, ANSI Z39.48-1984.

for Philip Winsor

Contents

Preface

Like *The Art of Translating Poetry* (University Park: The Pennsylvania State University Press, 1988), this book stems from my practical work as a translator and also from my concern to bring linguistic considerations, both practical and theoretical, to bear on the art of translation. As I said in the preface to that earlier study, "I have written this book to meet what seems to me an almost desperate need for some reasonably unified presentation of . . . the theoretical and linguistic and the practical aspects of translation." In essence, *The Art of Translating Poetry* argued that

1. No two languages having the same phonology, it is impossible to re-create the sounds of a work composed in one language in another language.
2. No two languages having the same syntactic structures, it is impossible to re-create the syntax of a work composed in one language in another language.
3. No two languages having the same vocabulary, it is impossible to re-create the vocabulary of a work composed in one language in another language.
4. No two languages having the same literary history, it is impossible to re-create the literary forms of one culture in the language and literary culture of another.
5. No two languages having the same prosody, it is impossible to re-create the prosody of a literary work composed in one language in another language.

These arguments, which perhaps sound overwhelmingly negative, take a good deal of their impetus from the *facts* of poetic translation. When it is attempted at all (that is, when translator and publisher do not combine to abandon all hope of transmitting one language's poetry as poetry in some new language, and therefore turn the quicksilver of verse into plodding prose), poetic translation frequently tries to translate what cannot be translated—rhymes, meters, forms—and ends, in the name of that will-o-the-wisp, "faithfulness," by stifling poetic vitality. In its theoretical as well as in its practical pages, *The Art of Translating Poetry* argues in favor of re-creation and approximation, rather than any struggle for a "literal" and "exact" reproduction, for all too often that struggle to preserve bones and skeletons succeeds in creating no more than a charmless, fleshless museum mounting.

But prose is a very different matter, with a very different history and, though not many of either its translators or its readers seem to know this, a very different linguistic nature. The translation of prose is therefore an exceedingly different business—and the usual *facts* of *its* practice are, once again, in largely direct opposition to controlling linguistic and literary realities. Translators of poetry (when, that is, they attempt poetic translations) are apt to squeeze their work into straitjackets, into largely outdated corsets and whalebones. The informed commentator on poetic translation thus needs to be an advocate not for license but for a spirited and intelligent relaxation. But translators of prose tend to be unaware that their originals have anything but a semantic existence. They translate "meaning" in its narrowest verbal sense—pretty much word-by-word. But as a close examination of the structures of prose reveals, it is by its very nature woven much closer to the syntactic bone than is poetry. Indeed, although poetry regularly and with gay impunity violates its language's syntax, prose cannot tolerate either such an intensity of syntactic irregularity or such far-ranging violations. What is part of the very woof and warp of verse is, in a word, death to prose—because prose that plays fast and loose with syntax is either bad prose, incomprehensible prose, "poetic" prose, or no prose at all, rolling completely off one definitional table and dropping onto another. The "prose poem" has become a recognized form in its own right, nor do I have any quarrel with it. (I have written some myself.) But prose cannot be adequately translated without close attention to its inner structures: for proper prose translation the necessary and desirable freedoms of the poetic translator must be curbed, for the basic component of prose style, as well as an important aspect of prose significance (meaning), turns out to be syntax.

The fundamental argument of *The Art of Translating Prose,* accordingly, is that proper translation of prose style is absolutely essential to proper translation of prose, and close attention to prose syntax is absolutely essential to proper translation of prose style. In literary prose, the style *is* the man (or the woman), the very sign and hallmark of the mind and personality at work on the page before us. In the translation of prose, therefore, to ignore or to maltreat style is to fail even before you begin.

This book develops that argument, fleshes it out with a host of examples,[1] and traces much of its history and its consequences—chief among which is the sad fact that few translators of prose, and even fewer readers, seem to have advanced much beyond Molière's "bourgeois gentilhomme," Monsieur Jourdain, and the Maître de Philosophie who instructs him. "Tout ce qui n'est point prose est vers," says the man of learning, "et tout ce qui n'est point vers est prose" ("Everything that's definitely not prose is poetry, and everything that's definitely not poetry is prose"). The conclusion that Monsieur Jourdain draws from this cheerfully circular definition is still, I suspect, the one that most people would unthinkingly (and mistakenly) draw, namely, that "il y a plus de quarante ans que je dis de la prose sans que j'en susse rien" ("I've been speaking prose for more than forty years and never known I was doing it").[2]

If only it were truly that easy!

---

1. See the Appendix for a brief discussion of how the various examples were selected.
2. Molière, *Le Bourgeois Gentilhomme,* II.iv.

PART

1

Tracking Syntactic Movement

Tain't what a man sez, but wot he *means* that the traducer has got to bring over.

—Ezra Pound

1

The Linguistics of Prose Versus the Linguistics of Verse

This being a study of translation *into* English, let me begin with an exercise based on translation *from* English. Suppose a document beginning with the nominal phrase, "The Internal Revenue Service..." The verb comes next; we stop before it appears, but as speakers and readers of the language we of course remain aware, without knowing what specific verb the document will employ, that something which does what verbs do in English is not only on its way but very likely to appear immediately: "the IRS objects, the IRS says, the IRS may feel," and so on. That is, not surprisingly, not only does syntax create structure, but long experience of the incessant repetition of structure (which is another way of saying "language acquisition") creates individual subjective expectations. Cultural patterns, in short, if not fully predictable, do at least tend strongly toward their own self-fulfillment. In English, the appearance of a nominal phrase tends to create the expectation that a verb will appear next, and that expectation tends to create its own satisfaction. A very high percentage of the time, the verb *is* what does in fact appear next.

And that the verb's immediate appearance is a broadly cultural phenomenon (that is, it is system-driven; in this case the system is syntactic) rather than a narrowly verbal one becomes plain when we consider "The Internal Revenue Service" as if it were nothing more than a mere assemblage of words. I have just pulled off my shelf the best and certainly the most linguistically oriented desk dictionary the United States has ever produced, the Random House *American College Dictionary.* This marvelously accurate reference (now out of print) defines the three principal words in our phrase as follows (I will not comment on the linguistic role of the particle "the," this being a book about translation and not an elementary linguistics text):

internal = "situated or existing in the interior of something"
revenue = "the income of a government" or, more broadly, "the return
    or yield from any kind of property; income."
service (noun form) = "an act of helpful activity"

Suppose a translator who knew (from whatever source) the *words* of the phrase, but not the cultural context that in fact shapes their meaning. He or she might understand "The Internal Revenue Service" as referring to some helpful government activity having to do with purely domestic—that is, *in*ternal as opposed to *ex*ternal—income. This would be fairly close to, but by no means exactly the right meaning. Americans do not associate the Internal Revenue Service with anything "helpful," nor does the IRS limit itself to domestic income.

Clearly, words alone do not carry meaning—or, at least, do not carry *enough* meaning. And, equally plainly, the more idiomatic (that is, the more culturally rather than verbally shaped) the phrase, the truer this becomes: "manger son blé en herbe," which if understood as a mere sequence of words seems to mean "to eat one's wheat in the blade" (which does not mean anything very much), is of course a French expression meaning "to spend one's income before one actually receives it."

If our phrase, "the Internal Revenue Service," occurred in a British rather than an American context, it would be transformed into "The *Inland* Revenue *Office*," and the culturally uninformed translator's problems would center around "inland" ("away from the coast") rather than "internal," and around "Office" as opposed to "Service." In French the relevant term would be *recettes fiscales* (tax receipts; so too in Italian the phrase is *revenue fisco*); in German it would be *Staatseinkünfte* (government income); in Dutch, *de fiscus revenue* (treasury revenue); in Spanish, *Delegación de Contribuciones* (tax office); in Indonesian, *Kantor pajak* (again, tax office; the loan word *kantor*—borrowed from Dutch—is worth noting). It is not hard to see, and seems unnecessary to trace, the small but important differences that occur as we move from one language's way of talking about tax collectors to the next language's way; cultural and linguistic historians properly make much of such differences, for they are ripe with cultural and linguistic significance(s) of which the translator needs, when he can, to be aware.

Culture (that is, system) is thus operating on our nominal phrase in two principal directions: first, as syntax, it shapes word order and sequence, and thus the basic movement of the language; and second, as lexicon, it shapes the meanings of words and phrases. Both directions are in operation at the same time, with approximately equal force; in prose as in speech neither does or can operate without the other; and both are among the variable elements that individual writers (or speakers) manipulate to form their prose (or speech) style. Style itself of course takes on meaning as well: once we know A's style, B's style of and by itself communicates to us, quite apart from B's lexicon or syntax, some of the ways in which B himself is unlike A. But style depends on, is indeed inter alia composed of, variable aspects of syntax and lexicon.

Of course, the same can be said of verse—but the proportionate importance of lexicon as opposed to syntax is different in the two forms, so that the dimensions and also the meaning of style are likely not to be the same in verse and in prose. "The Internal Revenue Service reports that tax receipts are somewhat smaller this year than during the same period in any of the three previous years." This would be one among the myriad possible complete forms of an English-language sentence beginning with our phrase—a sentence in prose, that is, for in verse neither sentences nor syntax in general have anything like as much significance.

> Be gentle with oranges, this year:
> The IRS hasn't left them much juice.

Emphasis naturally falls, in this just-concocted poetic counterpart to the hypothetical prose statement, above, on "oranges" in line 1 and on "juice" in line 2. But "oranges/juice" is not a sequence dependent on syntax (neither are poetic lines dependent on, though they may follow the shape of, syntax: poetic lineation is frequently rhetorical or musical, or even visual and spatial, rather than simply syntactic). If we use terms like "declarative" and "interrogative" to categorize prose sentences, what terms do we choose to describe "oranges/juice"? "Evocative"? "Image-carrying"? It does not matter, nor am I concerned to develop a new critical vocabulary. The linguistic frameworks of poetry and prose are obviously dissimilar.

And if we make the poetic sample even more "poetic," by employing more poetic devices, the dissimilarity between the two frameworks becomes still more pronounced:

> Be gentle with oranges, this year:
> It isn't bruises they fear
> But the tax man's craving for juice.

Adding rhyme to our concocted poetic bit, plus a metrical pattern, almost necessarily takes us still further from the dominance of syntax. There is (or should be) no surprise in this, for:

1. Poetry, as compared to prose, generally places greater emphasis on the *sound of language,* on its music and rhythm, and also employs a greater intensity of verbal colors of all sorts.
2. Poetry, as compared to prose, lays diminished emphasis on literal, linear *significance* and relies far more on metaphor and other indirect ways of meaning.

There are ranges of operation, to be sure, and some prose becomes "poetic," just as some poetry becomes "prosaic." (It is worth noting that both adjectives tend to be pejorative, though "prosaic verse" is more negative than "poetic prose," the latter sometimes being meant as praise rather than censure.) But prose comes closer to poetry precisely when it (a) takes on aspects of poetic expression not usual to it and (b) when it correspondingly gives up some of its syntax-based linearity. " . . . A stone, a leaf, an unfound door; of a stone, a leaf, a door. . . . O lost, and by the wind, grieved, ghost, come back again." This epigraph to Thomas Wolfe's novel, *Look Homeward, Angel,* is therein printed (in italics, and just before the start of chapter 1) as prose. It has however been reprinted (though not by its author) as poetry, and it clearly is more poetic, as it is also plainly less syntax-based, than usual prose. Alexander Pope's poetry just as plainly relies more on direct (and therefore more syntax-based) statement than do most other poetic corpuses: we are not startled to have Pope writing "An Essay on Criticism" or "An Essay on Man," though "essay" is a term we associate with prose, and we are not startled when the former poem begins " 'Tis hard to say, if greater want of skill / Appear in *writing* or in *judging* ill" and the latter begins "Awake, my St. John! leave all meaner things / To low ambition, and the pride of kings." And we are startled neither when Matthew Arnold begins his "The Scholar Gipsy" with a much less direct "Go, for they call you, shepherd, from the hill" nor when he begins his "Callicles' Song" (from "Empedocles on Etna") with an emphatic and unnatural inversion of English syntax: "Through the black, rushing smoke-bursts, / Thick breaks the red flame. . . ." As Arnold assures us, logically enough, "Though they may write in verse, though they may in a certain sense be masters of the art of versification,

Dryden and Pope are not classics of our poetry, they are classics of our prose." His rationale is even more to the point: Dryden and Pope's work is the poetry "of an age of prose and reason."[1] Arnold may not be our best guide to Alexander Pope, but he knows what goes with what: prose goes with reason, with order, with—in a word—syntax.

And the historical evidence strongly supports this view of the differences between poetry and prose. Every human culture of which we have any record, whether it be living or dead, has developed poetry. Poetry thus has a strong link with oral expression, since by definition every human culture has language and the primary form of language is speech. Not all human cultures, however, develop prose; only cultures (and languages) that develop a written subset of the spoken language can be said, again by definition, to have begun the long process of developing prose. Without exception, those cultures which do develop writing, and then develop prose, always evolve prose later than poetry and, further, find that the prose of their particular language attains heights of literary excellence (high-order clarity, as well as high levels of aesthetic accomplishment) later still. In the history of English, for example, writing was a borrowed skill, transmitted initially by the conquering Romans and perpetuated by the Church, but even without the necessity of evolving a written form entirely on its own, English did not reach consistently high levels of prose for almost a millennium. The Angles and Saxons and Jutes who occupied and transformed Celtic Britain brought poetry with them; there are some surviving Old English (or Anglo-Saxon: the terms are interchangeable) poems that might be datable as early as the seventh century A.D.; but English prose does not reach its literary peak until the fifteenth century and Sir Thomas Malory. Geoffrey Chaucer, a very great poet, is also the possessor of a singularly lame prose style.[2] Thus, except when it is used to present poetry, or to record actual speech, and the like, prose may logically and conveniently be defined as the written form of a language.

In our era, certainly, English prose has had more than enough time to evolve distinctly different conventions for such matters as indicating the end of a sentence (or what we call in speech an "utterance"), which in prose is signaled by a punctuation sign called a period but in speech is signaled, most usually, by a terminal juncture and a fairly large drop in pitch (and usually in volume as well). Like the prose of other languages, though in its own individual way(s), English prose has also developed its

1. Matthew Arnold, "The Study of Poetry," in *Essays in Criticism, Second Series* (London: Macmillan, 1888), 41, 42.
2. See Burton Raffel, "English Prose for the English Novel: The Beginnings," *Thought* 59 (December 1984): 402-18.

own set of important conventions, as necessary to written language as they are unnecessary in speech, such as capitalization, underlining, a whole range of punctuation signals, italics, and so on. And over the centuries of its development and use, though once again the fact is not generally understood, like the prose of other languages our English prose has settled on a vocabulary suited to its various needs as well as a syntax significantly different from that of speech. Thus, an excessively "bookish" person is said to and in fact does "speak like a book"—that is, to use a lexicon and generally to organize the language in ways inappropriate for speech but perfectly acceptable on the printed page. As a practicing attorney, I once heard a tax law specialist speaking on the telephone and wanting to find out whether the person at the other end had begun to look into some particular matter, actually say "Have you commenced to endeavor to ascertain whether . . . " This is not the lexicon of speech; there are native speakers of English to whom, though spoken clearly and plainly, words like these would be more or less incomprehensible. Because I wanted to verify the quotation from *Le Bourgeois Gentilhomme,* cited in the final paragraph of the preface to this book, I happen to have on my desk a volume of Molière's plays that features a condensed biography of that writer. The first paragraph of that brief biography contains the following sentence (which it would seem exceedingly strange to term an "utterance," for what manner of man or woman would ever actually utter it?):

> [The] salient facts in Molière's biography are that he was a seventeenth-century, Parisian bourgeois, with all that that position and inheritance imply in the way of common sense, love of work, love of family, clear judgment, and sober Epicureanism; that he received the best sort of training for a social satirist in his formal education and in his opportunities for the observation of all classes of society; and that he was able to serve a long apprenticeship as an actor and as an author in order to develop his dramatic technique.[3]

Nor is it any secret that millions of native speakers of English, though perfectly competent to say anything they need and choose to say, cannot make acceptable use of the language's written form, almost invariably for lack of the practical experience with that form which those who read a great deal acquire automatically. As prose almost always does, the written

---

3. *The Principal Comedies of Molière,* ed. F. K. Turgeon and A. C. Gilligan (New York: Macmillan, 1935), 1.

subset of English has become sufficiently unlike the basic spoken form(s) that functional acquisition of the written subset of our language must take place separately from and independently of functional acquisition of the spoken form(s). The capacity to use (write) and to understand (read) written English is thus no more guaranteed to native *speakers* of the language than the capacity to use and to understand German is guaranteed to native speakers of French. In a sense, accordingly (though the metaphor must be recognized as a metaphor and not pushed too hard), those who have by reading made themselves proficient in the written form(s) of English are practicing, when they read and also when they write, a sort of "translation," a transfer from one language to another. Just as a native speaker of English "studies" (or otherwise arranges for the acquisition of) German or French, so too the native *speaker* of English is no more automatically a native *reader* and *writer* of English than the native speaker of any language is automatically a native reader and writer of that language. The ideal way to learn another language is to spend time in places where that other language is used: France, for French; Germany, for German; and so on. The place where that different form of the language known as prose is used is, *tout court,* the written form—which means, most usually, newspapers, magazines, and books. And the person who spends time with newspapers, magazines, and books is usually occupied in reading.

To capture (translate) the written form (prose) of one language in the written form (prose) of another language is thus in distinct and absolutely inherent ways different from capturing (translating) the spoken (or the poetic) form. As re-creation of prose, translation is necessarily subject to all the differing conditions to which original prose is subject: as a purely linguistic phenomenon, translation differs from original creation only in its origins, not in its nature. Origins, that is, play immensely important roles in outcomes; the process of re-creating prose is exceedingly different from the process of creating prose *ab initio.* But as a linguistic outcome, the translation that is the end result of that different process is, again, shaped by and obedient to the same linguistic forces which shape and regulate any other prose in that same language, exactly as is the translation which is the end result of the re-creation of poetry in some other language. The linguistic forces themselves are different; their suzerainty is however the same. No translator of prose is or can be any more invulnerable to those linguistic forces than is the translator of poetry.

"That linguistic anarchy has its uses," says Walter Nash, "there is no doubt; and we have ingenious advocates for it, in the guise of specially-accredited persons enjoying a traditionally honoured privilege of living both inside and outside the [social] contract. Some of these inside-outsiders," he points out, "are comedians, clowns." But the poet, "too, is the outsider on the inside, the anarchist who relies on the conventions." And Nash then sets out, without any intention of exhausting the list, what seem to him the central aspects of the poet's "linguistic anarchy":

> He may take cavalier liberties with the syntax of the language, though he never pursues liberty to the point of total disorder; he proclaims, through word-play, image, and metaphor, his right to reassess the values of the lexicon; he may even triumphantly assert his privileged status with some turn of language that directly challenges one or other of the "terms" of our unwritten [social] contract.[4]

There is nothing startling or even new in this formulation. As Roman Jakobson wrote in 1935, "The essence of poetic figures of speech does not simply lie in their recording the manifold relationships between things, but also in the way they dislocate familiar relationships. The more strained the role of the metaphor in a given poetic structure, that much the more decisively are traditional categories overthrown."[5] More metaphorically, indeed, Jakobson deals with the differences between prose and poetry as akin to the differences between languages, referring to those who write both poetry and prose as "cases of . . . bilingualism."[6] We can if we like also say with Paul Friedrich that the issue "is not poetry versus nonpoetry but more poetry versus less poetry," for it is certainly true that in the broader senses of the words "poetic language permeates ordinary language, and also technical languages."[7] (To be sure, we are more likely to assume this latter perspective if our primary concern is, as the title of Friedrich's book makes clear, poetry rather than prose.)

Nor are the structural differences between prose and poetry dependent on the level of achievement in either form. For the most part, good and bad poetry are poetry, and good and bad prose are prose, as we can perhaps see most clearly if we look at Old rather than Modern English examples of each. The preface to King Alfred's translation of Gregory the Great's sixth-century *Cura Pastoralis* ("Pastoral Care") begins (with both "eth" and "thorn" represented by modern English "th"):

4. Walter Nash, *Our Experience of Language* (New York: St. Martin's, 1971), 92–93.

5. Roman Jakobson, *Language in Literature,* ed. Krystyna P. Pomorska and Stephen R. Rudy (Cambridge: Harvard University Press, 1987), 310.

6. Ibid., 301.

7. Paul Friedrich, *The Language Parallax: Linguistic Relativism and Poetic Indeterminancy* (Austin: University of Texas Press, 1986), 24.

ælfred kyning hateth gretan wæferth biscep his wordum luflice
ond freondlice. Ond the cythan hate, thæt me com swithe oft on
gemynd hwelce wiotan iu wæron geond angelcynn ægtherge
godcundra hada ge woruldcundra; ond hu gesæliglica tida tha
wæron geond Angelcynn; ond hu tha kyningas the thone anwald
hæfdon thæs folces gode on his ærendwrecum hirsumedon; ond
hu. . . .

Probably written between 890 and 896, this is plainly an early form
of English and just as plainly requires translation to be understood by
English speakers (and readers) of our own time. It is possible to render
this passage as follows:

King Alfred sends greetings to Bishop Wæferth with his loving
and friendly words, and would declare to you that it has very
often come to my mind what wise men there were formerly
throughout the English people, both in sacred and in secular
orders; and how there were happy times then throughout England;
and how the kings who had rule over the people in those days
were obedient to God and his messengers, and. . . . [8]

Alfred's prose, though better than much of that which has survived
from his time, is nevertheless not distinguished work; the translation
just quoted is thus for many purposes quite serviceable. But since it
seems fairly automatically to assume the right to smooth out and
modernize the structure of Alfred's prose, it reflects very little of his
style, thus depriving the modern reader of the opportunity fully to
track the king's mind at work. In the Old English, for example, the
first sentence ends after "freondlice" ("with friendship"). That is, for
Alfred but not for the modern reader the first whole syntactic unit,
eleven words long, is set off from what follows: "Alfred the king greets
Wæferth the bishop lovingly and with friendly words." The prose of
Queen Elizabeth I's time would have been far more likely to link this
greeting to what follows it, using a construction such as "would [i.e.,
"would like to"] declare to you that it has very often come to my
mind . . ."; the men and women of Elizabeth's day practiced exactly
that kind of decorous politeness. But the Anglo-Saxon mind is not the
Elizabethan mind, and to Alfred's way of thinking the greeting is mani-

8. *Anglo-Saxon Prose,* ed. and trans. Michael Swanton (Totowa, N.J.: Rowman &
Littlefield, 1975), 30.

festly not to be subordinated in this way, but is to stand, quite independently, at the start of his message. The greeting has a force and
a solemn meaning all its own: to subordinate it is to obscure that
fact beyond the modern reader's ability to perceive it. The translator's
principal other modernization is the replacement (smoothing out) of
Alfred's long series of coordinate clauses, each and all beginning with
ond (and) and most indeed beginning with *ond hu* (and how). I have
not reproduced the entire sentence in the Old English, for it runs
(in print) to fourteen lines, with eight iterations of *ond* (counting
the one at the start of the sentence, as indeed we should), six of
them being iterations of *ond hu.* The translator has, I should make clear,
tried to indicate most of this structure: in the complete translation,
which I have not quoted either, there are five iterations of "and how"
(though one of them practices the minor smoothing out involved in
replacing a semicolon by a comma). But whatever may be gained in "read-
ability" by thus diminishing the intensely replicative, piled-up structure
of the original, is I think more than offset by the loss of what that
structure tells us, first, about the state of Old English prose and, second,
about the movement of ideas in King Alfred's mind. Literary prose is not
simply the transmission of information in the most expeditious or comfortable mode. The *how* of that transmission is every bit as important as
the *what;* the medium, to borrow a phrase, is every bit as important
as the message, because in good part it too *is* the message. Just as
what we hear over the radio is not identical to the same words heard via a
television broadcast, so too a differently transmitted form of the same
semantic idea does not transmit the same message.

Although Old English as a language is no more highly inflected in
prose than in verse, what we see when we turn from Old English prose to
Old English poetry is, predictably, that syntax plays a very much smaller
role in shaping either verbal meaning or those subtler kinds of meanings
carried, in poetry generally, by sound, color, and the like. A relatively
straightforward bridge passage from the early, more or less expository
part of the epic poem *Beowulf,* for example, shows that alliteration plays
a huge role in deciding emphasis; that color words, adjectives and adverbs,
have in a sense more "muscle" than do verbs; and that the parallel
structures of verse movement also outweigh any structures erected for us
by syntax:

> Tha wæs on burgum Beowulf Scyldinga
> leof leodcyning long thrage
> folcum gefræge—fæder ellor hwearf,
> aldor of earde—oth thæt him eft onwoc

heah Healfdene; heold thenden lifde
gamol ond guthreouw glæde Scyldingas.[9]

An essentially word-for-word rendering, though unidiomatic, will perhaps better illustrate this point:

Then was in castle/palace/town Beowulf of the Scyldings
a beloved king [of the people] a long time
among the peoples well-known/renowned—[his] father elsewhere [to
    death] went
the chief/lord/prince from the land/region/home/dwelling—until to him
    in turn/afterwards was born
exalted/high/noble Healfdane, who ruled/guarded/possessed while/as
    long as he lived
old/aged and fierce in battle the lordly/gracious Scyldings.

No matter what approach verse translators may take, and I have deliberately chosen poetic translations of virtually every stamp, their work demonstrates the diminished importance of syntax:

Then Beaw held them   banished war-ravens
sailed through the summers   strengthening peace
like his father before him   known far abroad
a king to contend with.   Time brought a son
high-minded Healfdene   who held in his turn
through long glory-years   the life-line of Scyld.[10]

In the camps of the Scyldings as king reigned Beowulf;
dear lord of his people, for long he ruled,
and famed was afar when his father had gone,
the prince from the realm, till arose thereafter
Healfdene the mighty, who held while he lived,
fiercely battling till old, the happy Scyldings.[11]

Then Beowulf long was belovèd king
of the Scyldings, famed in the cities—
his princely father had passed away—
until to him in turn came Halfdane,

9. Lines 53-58.
10. Frederick Rebsamen (New York: HarperCollins, 1991).
11. Trans. Gordon Hall Gerould (New York: Ronald Press, 1929).

his great heir, who ruled the gracious Scyldings
till old, and ever bold in battle.[12]

Then in boroughs and towns Beow, the Scylding,
belovèd leader, through a long kingship
was most famed to his folk (his father had departed,
high prince from his homeland), until Halfdane, the Tall,
had been reared to rule. He reigned to his deathday,
agèd, but able, among his own people.[13]

That country then saw Beowulf of the Scyldings
Renowned among the people, a beloved king
Ruling many years—his father and lord
Having gone from the world—until there was born to him
Noble Healfdene; war-grim, aged,
Lifelong guardian of the illustrious Scyldings.[14]

Then Beo was king in that Danish castle,
Shild's son ruling as long as his father
And as loved, a famous lord of men.
And he in turn gave his people a son,
The great Healfdane, a fierce fighter
Who led the Danes to the end of his long
Life.... [15]

Not one of these six very different renderings either handles the syntax
in the same way or gives it anything like the controlling role we saw it
exercise in the passage from King Alfred's prose. Just as significant, in
their different attempts to give us the *poetry* of *Beowulf,* none of the six
present us with the same poem. Absent the strong regulating hand of
syntax, each of the six emphasizes different aspects of the original—and
this becomes still clearer if we set against these poetic renderings a set of
prose translations of the same passage:

Then Beowulf became the loved king of Scyldings in their fortress-
halls and had long fame among the folk (the prince, his father,
had turned away from home) until great Healfdane was born to

12. Trans. Stanley B. Greenfield (Carbondale: Southern Illinois University Press, 1982).
13. Trans. Ruth P. M. Lehmann (Austin: University of Texas Press, 1988).
14. Trans. Edwin Morgan (Berkeley and Los Angeles: University of California Press,
1952).
15. Trans. Burton Raffel (New York: New American Library, 1963).

him; he ruled the lordly Scyldings while he lived, old and fierce in fray.[16]

Then in that stronghold the beloved king of the people, Beowulf of the Scyldings, was for a long time famous among the nations (his father, the sovereign, having passed away from his land), until to him in his turn there was born Healfdene the Tall, who ruled the gracious Scyldings as long as he lived, and even as an aged man was fierce in the fray.[17]

Then in the cities was Beow of the Scyldings beloved king of the people, long famous among nations (his father had gone elsewhere, the king from his land), until later great Healfdene was born to him. As long as he lived, old and fierce in battle, he upheld the glorious Scyldings.[18]

Then Beowulf of the Scyldings, beloved king of the people, was famed among peoples long time in the strongholds—his father had passed hence, the prince from his home—until noble Healfdene was born to him; aged and fierce in fight, he ruled the Scyldings graciously while he lived.[19]

Then in the strongholds was Beowulf of the Scyldings, dear king of the nation, long time renowned among peoples,—the prince his father had gone elsewhere from the earth,—until the noble Healfdene was born to his home. While he lived, old and fierce in battle, he ruled the gracious Scyldings.[20]

Plainly, in the process of reducing poetry to prose, each of these five translators magnifies—and necessarily magnifies—the role of syntax. We seem to be reading now not a series of variations on a similar theme so much as five ways of saying pretty much the same thing. It is no accident—to return for a moment to our IRS example—that the statute that ultimately governs all income tax matters, and the IRS itself, is written in prose and not in verse. Nor is it accidental that when literary lawyers turn to spoofing the law they frequently turn to verse, a form of expression on its face unsuitable to legal clarity. Establishing the umbilical link

16. Trans. Lucien Dean Pearson (Bloomington: Indiana University Press, 1965).
17. Trans. G. N. Garmonsway and Jacqueline Simpson (New York: Dutton, 1968).
18. Trans. E. Talbot Donaldson (1966; New York: Norton, 1975).
19. Trans. R. K. Gordon (1926; New York: Dutton, 1954).
20. Trans. John R. Clark Hall (1911; London: Allen & Unwin, 1950).

between syntax and prose, which in turn depends on the umbilical link between syntax and meaning, makes it clearer, too, that, while conceding each form of expression its own logic, the logic we associate with prose is linear and the logic we more often than not associate with poetry is nonlinear. "Linear," says the *American College Dictionary,* means "extended in a line . . . involving measurement in one dimension only." Eviatar Zerubavel's study of "the history and meaning of the week," *The Seven Day Circle,* points out that "we often view time [itself] in the form of a line, a sort of arrowlike vector along which historically unique events are arranged in an irreversible order. This linear conception of time," he emphasizes, in fact "underlies our basic approach to history." But "time can also be viewed in the form of a closed circle. Essentially nonhistorical, a circular view of time revolves around the experience of *recurrence . . .* "[21] And as I have myself explained, "Poetic meaning is like and yet unlike ordinary meaning, just as poetry is both like and unlike ordinary speech or ordinary writing in prose forms. . . . The key, of course, is learning when we are dealing with what might be called literal meaning, and when we are dealing with what might be called nonliteral meaning."[22]

Given such completely basic differences between the nature of poetry and the nature of prose, we might better ask, it seems to me, how the process of translating poetry and the process of translating prose could *not* be different.

21. Eviator Zerubavel, *The Seven Day Circle* (New York: The Free Press, 1985), 83.
22. Burton Raffel, *How to Read a Poem* (New York: Meridian, 1984), 3-4.

2

Tracking Syntactic Movement
in Different Languages

Human meaning has often been confused with meaning per se—some absolute signification, both (a) inherent in creatures, objects, and events and (b) unchanging, even unchangeable. But as Bruce Gregory, associate director of the Harvard-Smithsonian Center for Astrophysics, has sought to explain, such absolutes, whether they exist or not, are quite simply unavailable to mere humans like us. "Physicists," he declares in the second paragraph of *Inventing Reality,* have "invented a language in order to talk about the world."[1] This is in no sense a metaphorical assertion: "The laws of physics are *our* laws, not nature's."[2] Or as the late Richard Feynman, a Nobel Prize winning physicist has said, "When we see a new phenomenon, we try to fit it into the framework we already have. . . . It's not because Nature is *really* similar; it's because the physicists have only been able to think of the same damn thing, over and over again."[3]

So too are human languages humanly constructed ways of dealing with the world, and like human science, or human dwellings, or human tools, or human clothes, these languages differ from place to place and from

1. Bruce Gregory, *Inventing Reality: Physics as Language* (1988; New York: John Wiley & Sons, 1990), v.
2. Ibid., 96.
3. Quoted in ibid., 166.

time to time. Like humans, they tend to aggregate themselves in consanguinity groupings: French is more like Spanish than it is like German, and German is more like English than it is like French, and Indonesian or Chinese are not much like French, Spanish, German, or English. Old French is more like its ancestor, Latin, than is Modern French, just as Old English (or Anglo-Saxon) is more like its ancestor, Angle-isc, than is Modern English. All Indo-European languages (English, German, French, Spanish, and Latin, among others) are more like each other than they are like, say, any of the Austro-Polynesian languages (Indonesian, Tagalog, Hawaiian). If as some linguists have argued there truly is some absolute human language, genetically transmitted, it remains and is likely forever to remain unrecoverable by mere humans. We must take it as given that, although we do not precisely understand how different languages come to be different, the differences between and among them are real and important, and deserve both high-order respect and close attention from those who attempt prose translation. Linguists indeed define "a language" as a form of speech that has its own rules and procedures and is incomprehensible to those who know only some other form of speech. (There also exist, *within* languages, "dialects," which are forms of speech partially but not entirely mutually comprehensible from one group of speakers to another.) Mutual incomprehensibility, therefore, is both the reason for and the special responsibility of translation.

But even though it is plainly impossible to deal with all known human languages or all the differences between and among them, it may be possible to claim universal applicability for certain aspects of such differences. Let me therefore start with the problems involved in translating prose from *bahasa indonesia,* or Indonesian, precisely because it is an Austro-Polynesian tongue about as unlike English—in syntax, lexicon, phonology, underlying cultural circumstances, and history—as a human language can well be. (Translation into English is inevitably my primary, if not quite my exclusive, focus; those who translate, say, from Indonesian to French, or from Indonesian to German, must necessarily deal with still different issues.) If there are aspects of syntax that can be tracked between two languages, one of which (English) can be characterized as "a synthetic language; it relies chiefly on inflectional morphology to indicate grammatical relations,"[4] and the other of which (Indonesian) can be described as containing sentences like "*harimau makan babi* 'tiger + eat + pig'... [which have] an infinite number of meanings, varying from 'tigers eat pigs' to 'the tigresses have eaten a boar,' "[5] then

4. *The World's Major Languages,* ed. Bernard Comrie (New York: Oxford University Press, 1990), 97.
5. Ibid., 928.

we can fairly assume that any such tracking is more or less equally possible between any two human languages known to us.

Since I would like, when possible, to deal with illustrative material that has a number of exemplars, and multiple versions of Indonesian prose in English translation are even harder to find than multiple versions of Indonesian poetry in English translation (poetry, being shorter, is inevitably translated more often, though "often" is of course strictly a relative term), I will take as my illustrative text a passage from Achdiat K. Mihardja's 1949 novel, *Atheis* (*The Atheist*), though I have previously discussed it, from a very different perspective, in my first book on translation.[6]

> Tapi, sore esoknya aku sudah menajung lagi menuji Kebon Manggu. Memang, manusia itu kadang-kadang bisa meloncat dari ujung keujung, berpindah niat atau penderian dengan sangat tiba-tiba. Tapi kenapakah sebetulnya bisa begitu? Hasil perjuangan batin? Apakah ini sebetulnya? Perjunangan perasaan? Perjuangan memauam? Ingatlah aku akan kata guruku, bahwa manusia itu selalu harus awas dan waspada dalam memperjuangan sesuatu dalam batinya, oleh karena katanya seringsering kita tidak tahu, bahwa kita sudah disesatkan oleh bimbingan setan. Hanya orang yang bermaksud suci selalu berada dalam bimbingan Tuhan. Maksudku suci. Aku yakin akal hal ini. Dan oleh karena itu yakin oula, bahwa aku berada dalam bimbingan Tuhan.[7]

This paragraph, which opens the novel's sixth chapter, records the inner struggles of a devout believer trying to deal with the temptations of the flesh. He is on his bicycle, riding (literally) toward temptation, though he tries to convince himself that his mission is a holy one. Since Indonesian uses essentially the same prose signals—punctuation markers, capital letters—to which English readers and writers are accustomed (having been printed in the Roman alphabet since 1907), it is easy enough to see, whether one understands the language or not, that there are thirteen sentences, most fairly short, one fairly long. Syntactic forward movement is interrupted, to use a decidedly gross measure of such things, by seven commas—a relatively small number for a passage containing thirteen sentences. There is also a string of six consecutive sentences

6. See Burton Raffel, *The Forked Tongue: A Study of the Translation Process* (The Hague: Mouton, 1971), 98-102.

7. Published in 1949, the novel was of course printed according to spelling conventions no longer operative in Indonesia. I have accordingly modernized the spelling, though I have not in any other way altered the words Achdiat wrote.

ending with question marks. There are no other punctuation marks: the hyphen, used twice in this passage, is morphological and as often as not is replaced by the Arabic numeral 2 (so that *tiba-tiba,* for example, is written *tiba2,* without signification being in any way changed). If, then, as I have been arguing, style is the mark of a writer's mind, and syntax (language structure) is a chief component of style, and it is the march of syntax which, carrying meaning on its shoulders, conveys to the reader the most basic and important things that a writer is able (or wants) to transmit, these bedrock syntactic facts are of crucial importance for any translator. There are in print at least four English versions, two drafted in 1963 by the late Jean Kennedy, one drafted by me in the same year, and the fourth by R. J. Maguire (who translated the entire novel) in 1972. Here is Jean Kennedy's first version, which like her other version did not please her; "I have translated [this passage] sixty different ways," she explained, "none of which amount to much. . . . In working over this passage I have gone from literal to free and back to strictly literal so many times that none of it makes any sense any more."[8]

> However, on the following evening I was pedaling again toward Kebon Manggu. I was thinking how men can occasionally jump from one extreme to another, switching their intentions or opinions quite suddenly. What makes them act this way? Is it caused by an "inner conflict"? What is the real reason? Is it a clash of ideas, feelings, or desires? I recalled my teacher's advice that one should always be cautious and conscientious when attacking a metaphysical problem because, according to him, frequently we don't recognize the devil when he beckons. Only the most virtuous are inspired by God. My aim in life was an ascetic one. I was positive of this and so I was positive too that I was in God's hands.[9]

Using gross measures, and without as yet commenting on the translation of specific words and phrases, we can see that this rendering reduces the number of sentences from 13 to 10, the number of comma-interruptions from 7 to 6, and the number of consecutive interrogative sentences from 6 to 4. Further: in Indonesian, the 6 interrogative sentences are without exception very short ones, containing (in this order) 5, 3, 3, 2, 2, and 2 words. This is definitely a pattern, and in no way accidental—

8. *The Forked Tongue,* 99-100.
9. Ibid.

which is made emphatic by the fact that the sentence immediately following the string of interrogatives is the longest in the paragraph, containing 32 words and 3 of the paragraph's 7 commas. The sharply marked contrast is surely of stylistic importance. Kennedy's first version, with only 4 consecutive interrogatives, gives us sentences containing (in this order) 6, 7, 5, and 9 words. The Indonesian's stylistic movement is obviously not followed. The relatively long sentence that follows does have 31 words, which is very close to the Indonesian number, but the contrast is doubly muted, first, because the difference between 31 and an average of 6.25 words is nothing like so stark as that between 32 and an average of 3.4 words and, second, because the sentence preceding the string of interrogatives contains 20 words in Kennedy's version and only 16 in the Indonesian. This latter discrepancy may not seem of much significance, being only a reduction of 4 words, but that is largely because the numbers involved are so small: it is in fact a reduction of 20 percent, a figure it is hard to think of as nonsignificant.

Here is Jean Kennedy's second version—and, again, remember that she was not only dissatisfied with these but with all her versions and did not go on to complete or to publish her translation:

> But on the next evening I was already pedaling toward Kebon Manggu. It's true, I thought, we sometimes go from one extreme to the other, changing our plans or opinions unexpectedly. What makes us act like this? It must be the result of "inner conflict." Beliefs, emotions, desires that are in conflict? I thought of what my teacher would say—that we should always proceed with care and caution when struggling with matters of the spirit because, as he put it, we are often led astray without knowing it. Only the righteous always have God's guidance, and because I was certain my aim in life was an ascetic one, I was certain as well that I had God's guidance.[10]

If the general tone of the first version is indecisive, the tone here is distinctly more consistent. A native speaker of English could, we suspect, have indeed written a paragraph like this, had this not been a translation. But that gain in coherence is purchased at the cost of a much greater departure from the syntactic movement of the Indonesian: consider the following brief table, listing first the figures for the Indonesian, then the figures for Kennedy's two versions:

10. Ibid.

	# of sentences	*# of interrog. sentences*	*# of commas*
Indonesian	13	6	7
Kennedy 1	10	4	6
Kennedy 2	6	2 [not consecutive]	9 (+ a dash)

"The style of the book, in Indonesian," as I wrote in a review of Maguire's translation, "is more subtle and flexible than the rather simple-minded narrative. The style, indeed, gives the book much of its literary value." I went on to term Mihardja's writing "nicely tuned prose."[11] Kennedy's second version gives us much more finely tuned, harmonious prose. But it seems, from our admittedly gross measuring rods, at the same time to be giving us something much less like the Indonesian original. Is this because English cannot, whether we want it to or not, be patterned on an Indonesian model? Are the fundamental differences between these almost totally different languages so enormous that no syntactic tracking is possible?

Here is the third version, produced by me in response to a request for translation assistance from Jean Kennedy, and produced (in 1963) with no knowledge of the rest of the novel:

> But there I was, late the next day, pedaling along the road to Kebon Manggu. It's true, people can sometimes hop from one extreme to another, suddenly taking new positions, following completely new roads. But why? Because of some inner torment and struggle? Really? A struggle of ideas? Or feelings? Or just desire? I thought of what my teacher would say: you have to watch this stirring around inside you, because words can lead us by the nose, Satan has led us astray before. Only a man with his mind set on holy things knows God's guiding hand. A mind bent toward holiness: that was me, surely. And because my mind so moved, wasn't I too led by God's all-knowing hand?[12]

With the exception of the number of commas, this version very closely matches the syntactic movement of the Indonesian. It has 12 sentences, instead of 13; the 6 consecutive interrogative sentences are here too, and with an average word count of 3.16, instead of 3.4—following, also, with an almost exactly matching long sentence of 31 (as opposed to 32) words; but the number of commas is much closer to Kennedy's second, more harmonious version, being a total of 9 and with two colons added.

11. *Books Abroad,* May 1974.
12. *The Forked Tongue,* 101.

There is also an extra interrogative sentence, at the conclusion of the paragraph, added, as I explained at the time, "because the guy obviously isn't as uncertain as he says he is. The double *yakin* [certainly]: he doth protest too much, methinks."[13] Since commas represent interruptions rather than full stops, and also because they are markers of a far more personal than fully structural nature, I am led to conclude (though I was at the time flying completely by the seat of my pants, knowing neither the novel nor, frankly, very much about translating prose) that in a general way, of the three translations thus far considered, this is the closest to the Indonesian in syntax and therefore, all other things being equal, in style. (Note that I do not say it is either the best or, God help me, the best that might be produced.)

Here, finally, is the fourth version, published in Maguire's complete translation of Mihardja's novel:

> The following afternoon, however, I rode toward Mangosteen Gardens again. Man, of course, can sometimes flit from one extreme to the other, deviating without warning from his resolutions and opinions. But why should it be so? Is it the product of inner torment, conflicting thoughts, conflicting experiences, conflicting desires? What's the real reason? I remembered my guru saying man should always be wary about striving for spirituality because, he said, we frequently did not realize the devil had led us astray. Only the heavenly-minded were beckoned by God. My intentions were holy. I was sure of this and thus equally sure I was in God's hands.[14]

There is remarkably little correspondence between the syntax of Maguire's translation and that of the Indonesian original. Maguire employs only 9 sentences, instead of 13; his sentences are a good deal longer than either those of the original or than those in any of the other translations. Instead of 6 consecutive interrogatives, we are given 3, and their average word length is just under 8, as opposed to 3.4. There are 10 commas. And because the general length of sentences here is so much longer, the "long" sentence following the interrogatives is, at a length of 28 (as opposed to 32) words, hardly a contrast at all. One of the interrogative sentences here contains 13 words; the sentence preceding the interrogatives contains 20.

The statistical analysis, though as I have said gross to the point of

13. Ibid.
14. Achdiat K. Mihardja, *Atheis,* trans. R. J. Maguire (St. Lucia: University of Queensland Press, 1972), 42.

crudeness, is nevertheless an accurate predictor. "Maguire's translation cap-tures remarkably little of the [original's] style," I wrote in 1974, though without any reference to the kind of syntactic comparisons here set out.[15] I do not need to repeat my entire review: the careful reader will, I suspect, have already noted that Maguire's prose is wordy, heavy, and (as I said in 1974) "flattened out and dulled." Nor is this a simple matter of sheer *number* of words. Indonesian is a pithy language; Mihardja's paragraph contains 101 words. But while Jean Kennedy's two versions contain 121 and 119 words, respectively, and mine contains 121, Maguire's has only 107. If sheer number of words, rather than the structure shaped by those words, were the deciding factor, Maguire's translation would seem to be the pithiest and, indeed, by far the closest to the Indonesian. Manifestly, it is not: structure (syntax) rather than sheer number of words is what matters.

Despite its enormous and too-often ignored importance, syntax is of course not the whole story. "Meaning"—in the fullest and most complete sense of the term—is the sum of factors we cannot always predict or even understand. "Tain't what a man sez, but wot he *means* that the traducer has got to bring over."[16] Who could know, to choose a few not-too-unlikely instances, that Mr. A. (for reasons good and sufficient to him) fairly explodes with anger at the very use of a particular word, otherwise innocent of unusual significance? Who could know that Mr. B.'s last conver-sational exchange, or the last document his eye happened to encounter, was a demand for the instant repayment of a fifty-thousand-dollar loan he had mistakenly assumed would not be called? *Undsoweiter:* in both its spoken and its written forms, language, like most cultural phenomena, is a bundle of complex and not always entirely controllable movements of emotion and information from one person to others. "Meaning" *is,* we might say, as meaning *does:* what Mr. C. understands by a remark or a document may well not be what Mr. D. understands, and so their actions (and reactions) may well be different, too. If a kingdom has indeed ever been lost for want of a nail, surely others have been lost (or won) by dint of some misunderstanding—a "no" that was intended to mean "yes," a "hurrah" that was supposed to mean "oh good God!" or "Heaven help us!"

Which neither advocates nor excuses miscomprehension of the origi-nal text by *translators. Tapi, sore esoknya aku sudah menajung lagi menuji Kebon Manggu,* the first sentence of the paragraph from *Atheis,* carries the strictly verbal meaning, "But/all the same/still, the next afternoon I was/there I was once more/again pedaling toward/in the direction of Kebon Manggu" [Mango Gardens—a geographical marker,

15. *Books Abroad,* May 1974.
16. Ezra Pound to W.H.D. Rouse, 18 March 1935, in *The Letters of Ezra Pound, 1907–1941,* ed. D. D. Paige (New York: Harcourt Brace, 1950), 271.

here, that the translator is usually better off not translating, like "Times Square" or "Picadilly Circus"]. But "meaning" having the variability just indicated, this ten-word sentence is nowhere near so straightforward as it may look—as, indeed, the four translations show, in their handling of the very first word, *tapi* ("but, yet, still, however, all the same"). Kennedy translates it as both "but" and "however," the latter rendering followed by a comma, the former not. I have translated it "but," and Maguire both renders it as "however" and also transfers it away from its initial position in both the sentence and the paragraph, a small but clear disregard of sentence structure and verbal emphasis. "But" in medias res has a very different force from "but" in initial sentence (or paragraph) position.

The translators part company even more drastically in their handling of the second word, *sore.* Here we enter territory controlled by custom and habit (that is, culture), rather than by mere lexicon. Most dictionaries will tell you, accurately enough as far as it goes, that *sore* means "afternoon" or "early evening." They will not tell you, because no dictionary can provide this much detail, that although *tengah hari* is usually translated as "noon" or "midday" (*tengah* = "middle," *hari* = "day"), one o'clock in the afternoon or even two o'clock, by Indonesian time, is still *tengah hari,* though decisively past noon to us. That is, in Indonesia, and thus in the Indonesian language, the divisions of the day are not coterminous with the divisions we make in the United States. Indonesian does have a way of limiting *tengah hari* to precisely and exactly "midday" or "noon," and that is *tengah hari rembang,* "high noon" (*rembang* = "peak, zenith"). Since Indonesian culture takes a very different attitude toward time and exactness, I have yet to hear this latter expression used, though I'm sure it sometimes is, under circumstances not hard to imagine. *Sore,* accordingly, is not in fact "afternoon" as we use the term, marking off the precise hours when, after 12:00 P.M., morning has ended and evening has yet to begin. Instead, *sore* is more like "middle afternoon," or "late afternoon," or "early evening." (*Malam,* "night," sometimes translated as "evening," usually indicates a time when darkness has well settled in, that is, when daylight is plainly done with.) Kennedy is therefore correct, though to my mind somewhat unhelpfully, when she twice translates *sore* as "evening." Americans, when they employ bicycles as their preferred means of transportation, tend to employ them in the daytime hours, and "evening" suggests, at the least, some diminution of daylight. Maguire's "afternoon" is better, though still not optimally precise; I have myself translated *sore esoknya* as "late the next day," knowing as I do that "afternoon" can mean "early afternoon," and that in the early afternoon Indonesians tend to be at home, resting away from the tropical heat, rather than pedaling bicycles anywhere.

Esok = *besok* = "tomorrow, the next (following) day," and all four translations concur. *Nya* is a particle of either possession or emphasis; it has no
true parallel in English, and more often than not can be disregarded, as all
the translations here do. But the fifth word in the sentence, *sudah,* is a
good deal more than a mere omittable particle. It is in fact one of the two
most frequently used tense indicators in Indonesian; the other, *akan,* suggests a future time, and *sudah* a time that has passed. Thus, *aku pergi* =
"I go" and *aku sudah pergi* = "I went"—though it must be conceded that
aku pergi also means "I went." (Indonesian tense indicators are not at all
like those of English.) Maguire's "I rode" is therefore narrowly correct. But
what *sudah* really indicates (means) here is more like "By late the next
afternoon I had already started to ride toward...," a signification that
Kennedy's second version more helpfully (*and* more accurately, yes) translates as "I was already pedaling," and my version renders by "But there I
was." Again, Indonesian tense indicators are not at all like those of English,
as Maguire seems to assume. "I was pedaling," in Kennedy's first version,
is thus closer to the author's meaning than the narrowly "accurate" straightforward past tense of "I rode." And the author emphasizes his true meaning
by immediately employing the word *lagi* (once more, again), which
Kennedy's second version and mine subsume under "already" and "there
I was," but Kennedy's first version uses, syntactically, much as the Indonesian uses it, immediately after the verb: "I was pedaling again." Once
more (*sekali lagi,* in Indonesian), Maguire weakens the emphasis by trans-
ferring "again" to the very end of the sentence, "I rode toward Mangosteen
gardens *again.*" (The syntactic insensitivity in this translation is in truth
exactly that insidiously pervasive; I do not know if it can be cured.)

Life is short, and books should be too: to take us through this paragraph in full detail seems to me prohibitively elaborate. The earlier
syntactic analysis demonstrated that, even when working between two
languages as different as English and Indonesian, a high degree of syntactic tracking is both possible and desirable; this more verbally oriented
analysis demonstrates much the same thing. That is, despite the enormous and almost unfathomable differences between two languages as
distant from each other as English and Indonesian, the *movement* of
syntax in the one language can be transferred to the other. Or, perhaps
more accurately, the *outline* of syntactic movement is transmittable
across linguistic boundaries: full and precise re-creation of syntax proper
is, as I noted before in summarizing the argument of *The Art of Translating Poetry,* [17] flatly impossible. *Apakah ini sebetulnya,* for example, can

17. See the preface, and *The Art of Translating Poetry* (University Park: Pennsylvania
State University Press, 1988), 14-16 and 37-50.

be decomposed into the following morphological parts—that is, the parts which, acting together, compose syntax: apa = "what"; -kah = an interrogative particle, thus turning *apakah* into a word indicating a question; *itu* = "that"; *se-* = "one, the same"; *betul* = "correct, exact"; and *-nya,* as already noted, is a particle registering, for the most part, possession or emphasis. In a dogtrot rendering, "Is that [i.e., question word + "that"] really true (the truth)?" "What's the real reason?," as Maguire and Kennedy's first (and inferior) version somewhat wordily have it. Kennedy's second version subsumes the entire question into a sentence that begins as a declarative and ends in a puzzled interrogative: "Beliefs, emotions, desires that are in conflict?" And my version, I think consistently, translates it simply as "Really?" That may not reflect precisely the words used in the Indonesian, but—thirty years later—I still maintain that it is the true *mot juste.* That is, it is what the author *meant.* And, there being no exact English syntactical equivalent for *Apakah itu sebetulnya?,* "Really?" seems to me to best and most accurately trace at least the syntactical outline.

So too the fourth sentence from the end: *Hanya orang yang bermaksud suci selalu berada dalam bimbingan Tuhan,* which again in dogtrot style runs: "Only man who always intends/plans purity/holiness is in/inside guidance/leadership [of] God." Here, Maguire's failure to work close to the syntactic outline of the Indonesian helps him slip badly. Jean Kennedy's first version is somewhat clumsy: "Only the most virtuous are inspired by God" wrestles *orang yang bermaksud suci* into a more or less acceptable but rather too loose "most virtuous," and "inspired" is just plain wrong. Further, *selalu* (always) seems neither to have been directly translated nor subsumed, as it of course can be, in other phraseology. Her second version is both closer to the shape of the Indonesian and better: "Only the righteous always have God's guidance," which I frankly prefer to my own rendering, "Only a man with his mind set on holy things knows God's guiding hand." "Hand" is justified by the "inside" sense of *dalam,* but "mind set on holy things" takes five words to accomplish what Kennedy does with two, "the righteous," nor has she had to subsume *selalu.* It stands out very clearly, as it does in the Indonesian. But Maguire somehow produces "Only the heavenly-minded were beckoned by God," which entirely loses the shape and thus the sense of the original. It is hard to credit translation this bad with much comprehension of the original's *meaning:* indeed, "beckoned by God" is one of those essentially meaningless constructions often and aptly called "translationese." That is, meaning more or less nothing, they are mere verbal cannon fodder, mattress stuffing, cotton batting; no one who is constantly aware that language is *working,* is *doing* something, and therefore must be *meaning* something, could have used such phraseology here. Maguire clearly shows that he knows what the words *maksud* and *suci* mean, qua words: he accurately translates the next sentence, *Maksudku suci* ("My intentions/plans [were] holy/pure"), as "My intentions were holy." What but a failure to track the shape, the movement, of the original could have led him to so mangle *orang yang bermaksud suci?* As my former colleague, Sheldon Wise, explained to Indonesian users of English, almost forty years ago, "The trouble is usually not that the general meanings of the words are not understood ... [but] that the words are used in the wrong situations."[18]

If the conclusions reached in this extended examination of translating literary prose from Indonesian to English are valid, similar results should be obtained by similar (though less protracted) examination of prose translated from other languages into English. Discussion of translations from only one additional language would be considerably less persuasive than discussion of at least two others; finality is, again, virtually impossible to achieve. Having gone very far afield in my first choice of language, let me now return to the Indo-European fold and take my texts from first French and then German, both of which are sufficiently unlike English and also unlike each other to buttress my conclusions and round out this chapter.

Guy de Maupassant's "La Parure" (usually translated as "The Necklace" or "The Diamond Necklace") begins with the following brief paragraphs:

> C'était une de ces jolies et charmantes filles, nées comme par une erreur du destin, dans une famille d'employés. Elle n'avait pas de dot, pas d'esperances, aucun moyen d'être connue, comprise, aimée, épousée par un homme riche et distingué; et elle se laissa marier avec un petit commis du ministère de l'instruction publique.
>
> Elle fut simple, ne pouvant être parée, mais malheureuse comme une déclassée; car les femmes n'ont point de caste ni de race, leur beauté, leur grâce et leur charme leur servant de naissance et de famille. Leur finesse native, leur instinct d'élegance, leur souplesse d'esprit, sont leur seule hiérarchie et font des filles du peuple les égales des plus grandes dames.

This elegantly shaped but straightforward prose, resolutely expository, wastes no time in getting right to the core of our unfortunate heroine's

18. Sheldon Wise, *Common Mistakes in English as Used in Indonesia* (Jakarta: Pustaka Rayat, 1955), 9.

background, position, and temperament. There is more, not a vast amount but too much to quote, about her unhappiness, her material and spiritual wants, and then de Maupassant swings into his story proper: "Or, un soir, son mari rentra..." ("Now one night her husband came home...").

Treating the two opening paragraphs as a kind of unit, comparable to the paragraph from Indonesian, discussed earlier, we find (using the same kinds of categorization) a total of four sentences, two in each brief paragraph. The shortest sentence is the very first (21 words), the longest (completing the first paragraph) is the second (38 words), and the third and fourth sentences, comprising the second paragraph, have 37 and 27 words, respectively. Maupassant thus employs a total of 123 words, with an overall average sentence length of 30.75 words. The two paragraphs are very similar in length, 59 and 64 words, and their average sentence lengths are 29.5 and 32 words. Clearly, there is not a great deal of variation in sentence length; what variation there is can be found more in the first than in the second paragraph.

Unlike the Indonesian example, however, which is twentieth-century and so more inclined to extremes, fonder of the alternation of quite short and relatively long sentences, our nineteenth-century French passage employs two intermediate internal division markers, the more emphatic semicolon and the considerably less emphatic comma. There are two semicolons, one in each paragraph; they occur in consecutive sentences, in the second sentence of the first paragraph and the first sentence of the second paragraph. There are a total of fourteen commas, many more than in the Indonesian; the commas are evenly distributed between the two paragraphs, seven in each, though not evenly distributed as between the individual sentences. Sentence 1 of paragraph 1 contains two commas; sentence 2 of paragraph 1 contains five; sentence 1 of paragraph 2 contains four commas (and a semicolon); and sentence 2 of paragraph 2 contains three commas.

The rhetorical tone of the French passage (again, we have not yet reached any issues involving meaning) is clearly quite different from that of the Indonesian one. This is much less dramatic prose, without any question marks, with no large differences in sentence length. It more or less marches, unhesitatingly, toward the establishing of social and characterological boundaries, providing the reader with both needed information and also, to be sure, preliminary plot-focusing.

Two translations should be sufficient. Here, first, is an anonymous version, reprinted in a large, double-columned and inexpensive edition from volumes apparently first published in England in 1903:

She was one of those pretty, charming young ladies, born, as if through an error of destiny, into a family of clerks. She had no dowry, no hopes, no means of becoming known, appreciated, loved, and married by a man either rich or distinguished; and she allowed herself to marry a petty clerk in the office of the Board of Education.

She was simple, not being able to adorn herself; but she was unhappy, as one out of her class; for women belong to no caste, no race; their grace, their beauty, and their charm serving them in the place of birth and family. Their inborn finesse, their instinctive elegance, their suppleness of wit are their only aristocracy, making some daughters of the people the equal of great ladies.[19]

There is some odd phrasing, here, particularly in the second paragraph, but for the moment we must pass it by. In the grossest syntactical terms, this exactly matches the French original, having two paragraphs and four sentences, two sentences to each paragraph. But the syntactical matching is not quite so exact, for though the total number of words is comparable (130 instead of 123), as is the number of words per paragraph (62 and 68, instead of 59 and 64), and the division in the first paragraph is quite closely parallel (23 and 39 words per sentence, instead of 21 and 38), the first sentence in paragraph 2 is significantly longer (43 words instead of 37) and the second sentence is a bit shorter (25 words instead of 27). The translation diverges rather similarly in its use of semicolons, too, matching the second sentence of the first French paragraph with one semicolon, but employing three semicolons in the first sentence of the second paragraph, instead of only one. And the translation diverges, once more, in its use of commas, replacing the French total of fourteen (seven in each paragraph) with seventeen, nine in its first paragraph and eight in its second. None of these are shocking divergences; we know that nineteenth-century English usage tends toward more elaborate, more formal punctuation. But divergence is divergence, and this rendering plainly features (again, all issues of meaning left for the moment to the side) a syntactic movement rather more involved and rather differently balanced than the French original.

Here then is a second translation, roughly sixty-plus years more recent, by Andrew R. MacAndrew:

She was one of those pretty, charming young women who are born, as if by an error of Fate, into a petty official's family. She had

19. "The Diamond Necklace," in *The Complete Short Stories of Guy de Maupassant* (New York: Walter J. Black, n.d.), 28a.

no dowry, no hopes, not the slightest chance of being appreciated, understood, loved, and married by a rich and distinguished man; so she slipped into marriage with a minor civil servant at the Ministry of Education.

Unable to afford jewelry, she dressed simply; but she was as wretched as a *déclassée,* for women have neither caste nor breeding—in them beauty, grace, and charm replace pride of birth. Innate refinement, instinctive elegance, and suppleness of wit give them their place on the only scale that counts, and these qualities make humble girls the peers of the grandest ladies.[20]

Apart from the fact that we almost seem to be reading a different tale, once again the syntactic tracking, on the grossest level, is exact: two paragraphs, each with two sentences. But though the total number of words is virtually identical to the total in the French original (124 instead of 123), the balance between the paragraphs, and among the sentences, is significantly different. In both the French and the first translation the second paragraph is longer than the first, by 64 words to 59 words, in the French, and by 68 words to 62 words, in the first translation. MacAndrew's translation has 62 words in each paragraph. Further, though MacAndrew's translation pretty well replicates the balance between sentences in the first paragraph (24 words and 38, instead of 21 and 38 in the French, and 23 and 39 in the first translation), in paragraph 2 the markedly longer first sentence (37 words and then 27, in the French, and 43 words and then 25, in the first translation) is translated in 32 words, and the markedly shorter second sentence is almost identical, having 30 words. This signals a large-order change. MacAndrew's use of semicolons and commas is more or less equivalent to the first translation's: he has 2 semicolons and a dash; the first translation has 4 semicolons. He has 15 commas, divided 8 and 7 between the two paragraphs, more closely matching the 7 and 7 division in the French than the first translation's 9 and 8 division and total of 17.

As I have said before, translation of prose is of course not simply a matter of syntactic tracking. Lexical and word-based considerations are of high importance. Indeed, it would be impossible, comparing these two translations solely on the basis of syntactic tracking, to judge between them. It is however possible, on an examination of syntactic tracking alone, to see larger divergences from the French in MacAndrew's transla-

20. "The Necklace," in Guy de Maupassant, *Boule de Suif and Other Stories,* trans. Andrew R. MacAndrew (New York: New American Library, 1964), 143.

tion (hereafter "MacAndrew") than in the first translation (hereafter "Unsigned"). And when we (at last) come to the words themselves, we can pretty easily see that here too MacAndrew's version is much further from the original. There is not much to choose from as between "young ladies" (Unsigned) and "young women" (MacAndrew) for *filles,* though I would myself prefer the simple and quite as accurate rendering "girls." But *famille d'employés* = "family of employees, clerk, salesmen," is much better translated as "a family of clerks" (Unsigned) than as "a petty official's family" (MacAndrew). More: individualizing the generalized *famille d'employés* as "*a* petty official's family" both eliminates a distinction drawn in the French and also introduces a possibly confusing note that does not belong. Our heroine, we are about to learn, in fact marries "a petty official," and there is some sense of "marrying up," in the French. MacAndrew's translation eliminates it. And by particularizing her background, as the French does not, MacAndrew may seem to be offering a signal that in truth is no signal at all: a reader who thereafter expects the story to amplify on this "petty official" will wait in vain, since no such character exists in the original.

These are smallish but important matters. What happens to sentence 2 in this first paragraph is rather more drastically aberrant. The social distinctions drawn in the French, expressed in terms of accomplishments that the heroine has no *moyen* (method, way, means) of achieving, are four in number: *connue* (known), *comprise* (counted, taken into account), *aimée* (loved), and *épousée* (married). Those of us who, while regrettably American, have nonetheless read Balzac, or even Thackeray, perfectly well understand what de Maupassant is telling us: three of the four social distinctions are closely reflected in the "known, appreciated, loved, and married" of the unsigned translation, and the fourth is not too badly mangled. But MacAndrew does badly mangle them, with his "appreciated, understood, loved, and married." This is modern American sentiment, rather than, as it is meant to be, classical French social climbing.

"She was simple" (Unsigned) is not a very good rendering of "Elle fut simple": the possible ambiguity of the adjective (simple mentally? or simple in lifestyle?) is unfortunate. "She dressed simply" (MacAndrew) is better. But *parée* = "adorned, ornamented, decked out," nor is it specifically addressed to "jewelry," so that to translate "not being able to adorn herself" (Unsigned), while somewhat ungraceful, is to stay a great deal closer to the French than "unable to afford jewelry" (MacAndrew). This latter translation, by too soon focusing on jewelry, also tends to make the story more of a monochromatic affair than its cosmopolitan author intended. *Malheureuse* = "unhappy, miserable," so that to translate "wretched" (MacAndrew), though a bit too strong, is almost as good as "unhappy" (Unsigned). But to omit any translation of *déclassée,* simply reproducing it, exactly as it is in French though now, as a non-English word, in italics (MacAndrew), seems to me a falsification of tone. It may also introduce some confusion, depending on how firm a grasp of the French word a particular reader may have. "One out of her class" (Unsigned) avoids any such problem, though it is not perfectly accurate: the French word surely signifies falling "below" one's class rather than merely "out" of it. Further: in English people "belong" to rather than "have" a "caste," so that "les femmes n'ont point de caste ni de race" is surely better as "women belong to no caste, no race (Unsigned) than as "women have neither caste nor breeding" (MacAndrew). Indeed, the usual meaning of "to have no breeding" is "to lack breeding, to be deficient in breeding"— that is, to have bad manners—and, if one takes "breeding" in that sense, here, as in all likelihood most readers will do, the translation has intro- duced an insult never intended by the author. More: to insert a dash at this point is to seriously interrupt the flow of the syntax, separating the second clause from the subordinating *car* (which in French carries even more strongly than does the English word "for" the sense of direct causal linkage: it is often best translated not as "for" but as "because"). And what MacAndrew's translation substitutes for the original French sequence, "*car* THIS, *leur* (their) THAT," is a prepositional phrase, "in them," which still further separates *beauté* (beauty), *grâce* (grace, prettiness, attractiveness), and *charme* (charm, fascination, enchantment) from the irrelevance for women of *caste* (caste, class) and *race* (race, ancestry), which irrelevance, says the author, allows feminine beauty, grace, and charm to flourish. Accordingly, the translation "their grace, their beauty, and their charm" (Unsigned) works a very great deal better than "in them beauty, grace, and charm." In addition, the French goes on to explain that these quintessentially feminine qualities "leur servant de naissance et de famille," are "serving them as (for) birth and family." To translate this as "serving them in the place of birth and family" (Unsigned) keeps the stylistic shape and movement of the French, whereas the rather blunt and flat version, "replace pride of birth," is both too abrupt and, lexically, unnecessarily condensed. *Naissance* (birth) and *famille* (family) were important enough to de Maupassant that he carefully spelled them out for the reader. If we are to favor one over the other, emphasizing "birth" and omitting "family," there needs to be some good reason for the change. Concededly, as I have been claiming for years, no translation *is* the original, and perfect identity is a will-o-the-wisp. But every translation surely ought to reflect the original, re-create the original, as closely as it possibly can, for it is also true that the translator is not the author.

"Refinement" (MacAndrew) is a better rendering of *finesse* (fineness, neatness, delicacy) than is "finesse" (Unsigned). But the rather clanking rendering of "sont leur seule hiérarchie" ("are their only hierarchy") as "are their only aristocracy" (Unsigned) is, for all that, infinitely better than "give them their place on the only scale that counts" (MacAndrew), which is apparently intended to be, but *hélas* is not, merely a different way of saying the same thing. The only scale that counts in what? in everything? and to whom? This exceedingly free rendering seems to me to raise more unanswerable questions than it provides adequate explanations. Nor is "humble girls" (MacAndrew) for *filles du peuple* (daughters of the people) a satisfactory translation; the straightforward "daughters of the people" (Unsigned) much more accurately and clearly reflects the original, allowing the reader the kind of class information the author intended to provide. Finally, "peers" (MacAndrew) for *égales* (equals) is once again ambiguous, since in this context "peers" has an additional set of meanings, concerned with actual aristocrats, which have no place here; the straightforward "equal" is far better. Finally, either "grandest ladies" (MacAndrew) or "great ladies" is satisfactory for *plus grandes dames* (the greatest, loftiest, grandest ladies), since *grande* can have either meaning.

What we have thus found, perhaps surprisingly, is that the older, stiffer, more "literary"-sounding translation is both syntactically and stylistically, and also lexically, closer to the original French. The modern, free-flowing, and more "readable"-seeming translation by MacAndrew is syntactically and stylistically, as it is also lexically, considerably less representative of the original French. Neither version is entirely satisfactory; neither fully re-creates the original, as a good translation should. And though it is plainly not the sole indicator, once again failure to track the original's syntax is clearly a marker, a signal of failure to properly represent other aspects of the original.

For our third text, let me set out the first paragraph of Heinrich Heine's *Die Harzreise* (1824), "The Journey to the Harz," a dashing (and frequently slashing) account of a trip to the Harz mountains taken during the young Heine's legal studies at the University of Göttingen. "With *The Journey to the Harz*," as Frederic Ewen has noted, the not yet thirty-year-old Heine, still little known as a poet, immediately "established himself as a great German prose writer."[21]

> Die Stadt Göttingen, berühmt durch ihre Würste und Universität, gehört dem Könige von Hannover und enthält 999 Feuerstellen, diverse Kirchen, eine Entbindungsanstalt, eine Sternwarte, einen

21. *The Poetry and Prose of Heinrich Heine,* ed. Frederic Ewen (New York: Citadel, 1948), 19.

Karzer, eine Bibliothek und einen Ratskeller, wo das Bier sehr gut ist. Der vorbeifliessende Bach heisst "die Leine", und dient des Sommers zum Baden; das Wasser ist sehr kalt und an einigen Orten so breit, dass Lüder wirklich einen grossen Anlauf nehmen musste, als er hinüber sprang. Die Stadt selbst ist schön und gefällt einem am besten, wenn man sie mit dem Rücken ansieht. Sie muss schon sehr lange stehen, denn ich erinnere mich, als ich vor fünf Jahren dort immatrikuliert und bald darauf konsiliiert wurde, hatte sie schon dasselbe graue, altkluge Ansehen, und war schon vollständig eingerichtet mit Schnurren, Pudeln, Dissertationen, Thee dansants, Wäscherinnen, Kompendien, Taubenbraten, Guelfenorden, Promotionskutschen, Pfeifenköpfen, Hofräten, Justizräten, Relegationsräten, Profaxen und anderen Faxen. Einige behaupten sogar, die Stadt sei zur Zeit der Völkerwanderung erbaut worden, jeder deutsche Stamm habe damals ein ungebundenes Exemplar seiner Mitglieder darin zurückgelassen, und davon stammten all die Vandalen, Friesen, Schwaben, Teutonen, Sachsen, Thüringer, u.s.w., die noch heutzutage in Göttingen, hordenweis und geschieden durch Farben der Mützen und der Pfeifenquäste, über die Weenderstrasse einherziehen, auf den blutigen Walstätten der Rasenmühle, des Ritschenkrugs und Bovdens sich ewig untereinander herumschlagen, in Sitten und Gebräuchen noch immer wie zur Zeit der Völkerwanderung dahinleben, und teils durch ihr Duces, welche Haupthähne heissen, teils durch ihr uraltes Gesetzbuch, welches Komment heisst und in den *legibus barbarorum* eine Stelle verdient, regiert werden.

The movement of Heine's prose is manifestly unlike the passages from Indonesian and French already considered. This is of course partly because Heine is neither Achdiat Mihardja nor Guy de Maupassant; it is also because German syntax follows very different patterns from those of either Indonesian or French. To use the same essentially gross measures employed in analyzing the earlier passages: this almost page-long introductory paragraph contains only five sentences; the shortest of them are not truly short (17, 35, and 37 words, though not in this order), and the longest are rather elaborately extended (53 and 109 words), syntactic movement being regulated, as well, by no fewer than fifty commas. There is one semicolon; there are no other movement-controlling marks (the pair of quotation marks having nothing to do with syntactical movement). Words in German are not formed precisely as are words in either French or Indonesian, but in a crude measuring scheme we can reasonably neglect such considerations. (I have here largely but not completely modernized a nineteenth-century printing, so there would be still other discrepancies, were the scheme more rigorous.)

What matters, again, is how well the translations of this passage track the original's syntactic flow. Our first rendering, by Francis Storr, dates from 1887. (Note that, both here and in the third translation, below, I have inserted footnotes into the text, at the point where they are meant to be read, but have not counted them as part of the verbal total. Like most punctuation signals, translators' footnotes are interruptions of the syntactic flow.)

> The town of Göttingen, so celebrated for its sausages and university, belongs to the King of Hanover, and contains 999 inhabited houses, various churches, a lying-in hospital, an observatory, a university prison, a library, and a town hall tavern, where the beer is excellent. The stream that flows past the town is the Leine, and serves in the summer for bathing. The water is very cold, and in some places it is so broad that Panto had to take a really good run to clear it. The town itself is pretty, and presents the most agreeable aspect—when we have turned our backs upon it. Of its antiquity there can be no doubt, for I remember when I matriculated there five years ago (just before I was requested to take my name off the books), it had the same grey knowing look that it has now, and was as fully provided with Charleys* [*night-watchmen], beadles, dissertations, *thés dansants*, washerwomen, cram-books, pigeon-pies, Guelfic orders, graduates' visiting coaches, pipe-bowls, court-councillors, law-councillors, rustication councillors, bull-dogs, and other sad dogs. Some authorities actually maintain that the town dates from the days of the barbaric invasions, and according to them each German tribe dropped on its way a rough copy of itself, which accounts for all the Vandals, Frisians, Swabians, Teutons, Saxons, Thuringians, etc., who may be found in Göttingen even to the present day. Our young barbarians still go in hordes, and you may distinguish them by the colours of their caps and pipe-tassels. They lounge along the Weenderstrasse on their way to the sanguinary battlefields of Rasenmühle, Ritchenkrug, and Bovden, where they are always pitching into one another. Their manners and customs are survivals from the age of the barbaric invasions, and they are governed partly by their *Duces* (prize cocks they style them), partly by their primitive code styled the *Comment*. It well deserves a place among the *leges barbarorum*.[22]

22. "A Tour in the Harz," in *Prose and Poetry by Heinrich Heine* (London: Dent, 1934), 175.

As before, lexical aspects of this (and the other translations) will be discussed later. In gross syntactic terms, Storr's rendering gives us nine sentences (instead of five). None is remarkably short, which might seem to reflect at least some semblance of the syntactic movement of the German original, but the pattern of distribution is totally changed. Column 1 shows the sequence of sentence word-lengths[23] in the German; column 2 shows the same sequence in Storr's translation:

Heine	Storr
37	44
35	16
17	25
53	19
109	84
	54
	20
	25
	43

Even allowing for unavoidable changes in translating from a language like German, which is so much more apt to agglutinate words into ever-larger words, it is obvious that the flow of the translation is utterly different. If the argument of this chapter is correct, so complete a shift in syntactic flow should condemn the translation virtually out of hand. There is no way that so extraordinary a change can give even the slightest idea of Heine's style and/or the thought-progression within it. It is not necessary to concern ourselves with the fact that the translation uses no semicolons and the original uses one, or that the translation uses two pairs of parentheses and the original none. There are, for the record, forty-five commas in the translation; there are, again, fifty in the original.

A second translation is called for, and a third, before we can frame an answer to the central question: are these changes inherent in the differing natures of German and English? or are they simply a reflection of different approaches to translation? Here then is Frederic Ewen's 1948 rendering:

> The town of Göttingen, famous for its sausages and university, belongs to the King of Hanover, and contains 999 habitations, various churches, a lying-in hospital, an observatory, a student jail, a library and a Rathskeller where the beer is excellent. The

23. Translating German *words* into English *words* is not an exact process; these word counts are necessarily approximate rather than exact. Further, there are many more words in the translation than in the original—330 instead of 251.

stream which flows past the town is called the Leine, and in the summer is used for bathing. Its water is very cold, and in some places so broad that my schoolmate Lüder had to take quite a run to clear it. The town itself is beautiful, and most agreeable— when you have turned your back upon it. It must be very old, for I remember when I matriculated there five years ago, and was soon thereafter expelled, it already had the same grey, sage look, and was fully provided with watchmen, poodles, dissertations, *thé-dansants,* laundresses, compendiums, roasted pigeons, Guelfic orders, graduates' carriages, pipe-bowls, court councillors, law councillors, deans' counsellors, old fossils, and other imbeciles. There are those who even assert that the town was founded at the time of the Great Migrations, and that every German tribe had left an unbound copy of its stock behind, from whom all the fraternities like the "Vandals," "Frisians," "Suabians," "Teutons," "Saxons," "Thuringians," etc. are descended, who to this day wander through Weender Street in hordes, distinguished by the color of their caps and pipe tassels, fight incessantly on the bloody battlefields of Rasenmühle, Ritschenkrug, and Bovden, preserving the manners and customs of the barbaric invasions, and are governed partly by their *duces,* called "prize-cocks," and partly by their ancient code, called the "Comment," which well deserves a place among the *leges barbarorum.*[24]

There are six sentences in this version, instead of the original's five. To make clear that the translation tracks the original, here is a comparative table, showing the word lengths of the sentences in the German and in the translation:

Heine	*Ewen*
37	40
35	19
17	24
53	16
109	58
	115

Although we will again postpone for the moment lexical discussion, it must be remarked (since it is quite obvious) that there is a considerable

24. "A Journey to the Harz," in *The Poetry and Prose of Heinrich Heine,* ed. Frederic Ewen, 355-56.

difference between Ewen's and Storr's understanding of individual words and phrases (some but by no means all of which difference can, however, be attributed to the time-span between the two translations and to the fact that Storr was British and Ewen an American). But even without lexical analysis, the care with which Ewen has approximated the syntactic movement of the German should, if my argument is valid, dispose us to trust his sense of lexicography too. It is worth noting that the overall word count of Ewen's translation is much closer to that of the German: 272 in Ewen, 251 in German—and 330 in Storr. Ewen uses one dash, no semicolons, and no parentheses. His version employs forty-nine commas, instead of Storr's forty-five and the German original's fifty.

And so to a 1973 translation by Helen M. Mustard:

> The town of Göttingen, famous for its sausages and university, belongs to the King of Hanover and contains 999 dwellings, various churches, a maternity hospital, an observatory, a prison, a library, and a Ratskeller where the beer is very good. The brook flowing past is the Leine, and in summer it serves for bathing; the water is very cold and in some places so wide that Lüder* [*A student at Göttingen noted for his gymnastic prowess] really had to take an enormous running start when he jumped across it. The town itself is very beautiful, and most pleasing of all when viewed with one's back to it. It must have existed for a very long time, for I remember when I matriculated there five years ago, only to be expelled soon afterward, it already had the same hoary, knowing appearance and was already completely supplied with nightwatchmen, beadles, dissertations, tea dances, laundresses, cyclopedias, roast pigeons, Guelfic orders, carriages for graduating doctoral candidates, pipe bowls, *Hofräte*† [†Plural of *Hofrat,* an honorary title with no English equivalent], councillors of justice, councillors for expulsion, bibliomaniacs, and other maniacs. Some even maintain that the town was built during the migration of the Germanic tribes, that every tribe left there an unbound sample of its members, and from these descended all the Vandals, Frisians, Swabians, Teutons, Saxons, Thuringians, and so on, who still roam in hordes down Weende Street in Göttingen today, distinguished only by the color of their caps and pipe tassels, are forever fighting among each other on the bloody battlefields of the Rasenmühle‡, the Ritschenkrug‡ [‡Favorite duelling places of the students], and Bovden§ [§Bovden is a village not far from Göttingen], are still living according to the manners and customs of the age of the migrations, and are governed partly by their

duces, who are called cocks of the roost, partly by their ancient law-book, which is called "Students' Code" and deserves a place among the *legibus barbarorum*‖ [‖*Laws of the barbarians*].[25]

Mustard's version has five sentences (as well as five footnotes, which as noted earlier I have reproduced in the text proper: again, though strictly speaking external to the text, their presence, and especially in such numbers, cannot help but affect syntactic flow). The gross pattern of distribution is even closer to the German than is Ewen's:

Heine	Ewen	Mustard
37	40	40
35	19	40
17	24	18
53	16	68
109	58	128
	115	

However, though not so swollen as Storrs' (330), Mustard's total word count (294) is significantly higher than Ewen's (272). Mustard employs one semicolon, as does the original, forty-six commas, and has neither dashes nor parentheses. Again, if the grossly predictive measures I have been employing are accurate, when we now turn to the second principal aspect of prose translation—lexicon—we should find that, in this too, Mustard's and Ewen's translations are superior reflections of Heine's German; that Storr's understanding of German words is as shaky as his perception of German syntactic movement; and that the tracking of syntactic flow is, in and of itself, not a sufficiently powerful standard by which to judge between Mustard's and Ewen's versions. That is, a gross measure remains exactly that: gross. That which measures grossly is unlikely also to measure more finely. This necessary limitation has nothing to do with linguistic accuracy, stemming as it does from the complexity both of literary prose and of the translation of literary prose.

It may seem to an academic that Heine begins in a "rather nasty" style; "the scorn heaped upon the university town is ill-humored, and the undeniable wit of the opening passage . . . is constantly threatened by lapses into mere crudity."[26] Other poets do not agree: "Oxford is not intellectually stimulating," wrote T. S. Eliot at about the same age as

25. "The Harz Journey," in Heinrich Heine, *Selected Works,* ed. Helen M. Mustard (New York: Random House, 1973), 4–5.

26. Jeffrey L. Sammons, *Heinrich Heine, the Elusive Poet* (New Haven: Yale University Press, 1969), 105.

Heine was, when writing *Die Harzreise,* "—but that would be a good deal to ask of a university atmosphere."[27] Heine's verbal sequence—that is, the rapid-fire juxtapositions he effects—is dexterously comic: *die Stadt Göttingen* (the town/city of Göttingen) is *berühmt* (famous, celebrated, renowned) for its *Würste* (sausages) and its *Universität* (university). Ewen and Mustard nicely preserve the swift, merciless sarcasm, translating (identically) "Famous for its sausages and university." Storr, much less trusting of the original in matters of syntactic movement, immediately shows himself to be similarly less trusting lexically, leaning on the horn, as it were, by translating "so celebrated for its sausages and university." Verbosity is verbosity, whether expressed syntactically or lexically—and Heine's rapier-like wit suffers some significant diminution. Pretty much the same thing happens with *Feuerstellen* (fireplaces, hearths), translated interpretatively but succinctly by Ewen as "habitations" and by Mustard as "dwellings," but rather dragged out by Storr as "inhabited houses." Then the three versions are essentially equal, for a bit, though *Karz* has a clear student/university association and is better translated "a student jail" (Ewen) or even, more stiffly, as "a university prison" (Storr), than simply as "a prison" (Mustard). But though "town-hall cellar" (Storr) may be historically accurate for *Ratskeller* (town hall tavern), it has no clear meaning, and "Ratskeller" (or "Rathskeller") has since Storr's day come to be an acceptable English-language usage. "Where the beer is excellent" (Storr and Ewen) is not so good a rendering for "wo das Bier sehr gut ist" as the straightforward "where the beer is very good" (Mustard).

If the first sentence already shows the lexical deficiencies of Storr's translation, those deficiencies soon thereafter become glaring. So far as I am aware, the word "Ponto"—Storr's translation of the name *Lüder*—does have a slang meaning, in British usage, but that slang meaning (bread pellets thrown at one another by schoolboys) does not here apply. "My schoolmate Lüder" (Ewen) or the footnote employed by Mustard are translations that make sense; "Ponto" does not. And if the original makes sense, so too should the translation. *Wirklich* (really) is translated by Storr and Mustard but omitted by Ewen; it should not be omitted. *Einen grossen Anlauf* (a large-ish run) is more or less approximated by all three versions, as is the obligatory nature of *musste* (had to), but only Mustard gives us an unequivocal "jumped across" for *hinüber sprang;* "to clear it," used by both Storr and Ewen, is not as neatly precise. On the other hand, Ewen best handles the deft unpleasantness of "Die Stadt selbst ist schön und gefällt einem am besten, wenn man sie mit dem

---

27. T. S. Eliot to Eleanor Hinkley, 14 October 1914, in *The Letters of T. S. Eliot,* ed. Valerie Eliot (New York: Harcourt, Brace, Jovanovich, 1988), vol. 1, 61.

Rücken ansieht" ("The town itself is pretty/lovely/beautiful/nice, and best of all when it's your back that's looking at it"): not accidentally, there is a very good matching of syntactic movement, as well as a good lexical matching, in "The town itself is beautiful, and most agreeable—when you have turned your back upon it." Storr is excessively wordy here, and wordiness does not suit witty prose: "The town itself is pretty, and presents the most agreeable aspect—when we have turned our backs upon it." Since English does not have the convenient third-person *man,* either "you" (Ewen) or "one" (Mustard) is a better rendering than "we" (Storr). But Mustard's rendering here is too heavily blunt: "The town itself is beautiful, and most pleasing of all when viewed with one's back to it." Since the German has three phrases, and most closely links phrases 1 and 2, Storr and Ewen gain by doing the same thing, and Mustard loses by linking, instead, phrases 2 and 3.

"Dasselbe graue, altkluge Ansehen" ("the same grey/grizzled/hoary/ colorless/sombre, old-wise/knowing appearance") is rather minimally translated "the same grey knowing look" (Storr)—"minimally," that is, because the narrow accuracy of these words, lexically speaking, does not compensate for their rhetorical flatness. "The same hoary, knowing appearance" (Mustard) better says what Heine means; "the same grey, sage look" (Ewen) seems to me to carry Heine's meaning better still. All three translations struggle with the first of Heine's several barbed "laundry lists." (Is there any language better suited for barbed laundry lists than German?) Says the German, hilariously, "Schnurren, Pudeln, Dissertationen, Thee dansants, Wäscherinnen, Kompendien, Taubenbraten, Guelfenorden, Promotionskutschen, Pfeifenköpfen, Hofräten, Justizräten, Relegationsräten, Profaxen und anderen Faxen" ("nightwatchmen, university beadles [minor officials/poodles/drudges], dissertations, *thé dansants* [French: tea-dance/tea-party with dancing], washerwomen/laundresses, compendia, roast pigeons/pigeon-pies, Guelfic orders [from the warring medieval factions, the Guelphs and the Ghibellines], university graduates'/doctoral candidates' coaches, pipe-bowls, Privy Councillors, King's [or Queen's] Counsel, expulsion councillors, prose-writers and other idiots."). There is not a great deal of difference between and among the three translations, here or in the later laundry lists, though Ewen does explain the possibly bewildering reference to barbarian hordes, *hordenweis,* as a list of "fraternities." A nineteenth-century translator could assume enough Latin to use *duces* for "leaders"; even the relatively recent historical figure of Mussolini, known in Italy as "Il Duce," would not I suspect help most twentieth-century readers. The particulars of nineteenth-century German university life, a life now vanished from the earth, are difficult to reconstruct in another language and another time. Still, to translate *uralt* (very old, ancient, primeval) as "ancient" (Ewen and Mustard) is preferable to translating it as "primitive" (Storr) and thus imposing a value judgment not present in the original. To assert *any* value judgment, indeed, conflicts with the witty insults Heine is administering: the insult itself is quite sufficiently damning.

There is no need to prolong this verbal analysis unnecessarily. It seems clear, once more, that the predictive value of syntactic tracking as a measure is about what might have been expected. The final appraisal of the three translations, even were we to go into truly painful detail, would remain more or less where our analysis of syntactic tracking left it. Much more could be said, but little more would be gained.

3

Famous and Infamous Translations
Madame Bovary, Decameron

With the distinction between verse and prose clearly established, and the importance of syntactical tracking for the translation of prose at least signaled, if not absolutely proven, it seems appropriate to consider next a heterogeneous group of famous and infamous prose translations, to test still further the validity of syntactical tracking as an evaluative (and predictive) measure. Thereafter, we can appropriately conclude the book by considering, in some detail and from both theoretical and practical perspectives, the translation of two classic prose texts (both of which I have myself translated), Rabelais's *Gargantua and Pantagruel* and Cervantes' *Don Quijote*.

Since the treatment of literary style is central to effective translation of prose, and since Gustave Flaubert—especially in his greatest book, *Madame Bovary*—has been well known for more than a century as "the impeccable and patient polisher of sentences,"[1] some of the good, bad, and indifferent Englishings of *Madame Bovary* are virtually a perfect place to begin. "I have abscesses of style," Flaubert wrote to Louise Colet, as he was settling into the book, "I itch with sentences that never appear."[2]

1. Henri Peyre, *The Failures of Criticism* (Ithaca: Cornell University Press, 1967), 111.
2. Quoted from Francis Steegmuller, *Flaubert and Madame Bovary,* rev. ed. (New York: Farrar, Straus & Giroux, 1968), 237.

"No one has ever taken more pains than I. . . . Oh, what a slippery cus-
tomer style is!"[3]

We can begin, as Flaubert had to, at the beginning:

> Nous étions à l'étude, quand le Proviseur entra, suivi d'un *nouveau*
> habillé en bourgeois et d'un garçon de classe qui portait un
> grand pupitre. Ceux qui dormaient se réveillèrent, et chacun se
> leva, comme surprise dans son travail.

The chiseled understatement of Flaubert's style (André Gide referred
to "the perfection of the paragraph in Flaubert's prose"[4]) is packed
into two delicately balanced sentences. Each opens with a pair of short
clauses, pegged into place with a pair of commas, the first of each
pair having, in both cases, five words, the second of each pair having
four. But where the second sentence (and the paragraph) ends with
yet another five-word phrase, the first sentence eventuates in a slightly
longer-breathed utterance, marked by no signs of punctuation and con-
sisting of a seven-word phrase linked by the coordinating conjunction
et (and) to a still longer ten-word phrase. The weight of the paragraph thus falls, as also its sense turns, on these two longer phrases,
the key words of the first phrase being *nouveau* (newcomer) and
en bourgeois ([dressed] in plain/civilian/common style), the key words
of the second phrase being *garçon de classe* (classroom servant) and
grand pupitre (big/bulky writing-desk). To be sure, such syntactic
positioning does not, in and of itself, carry the entire meaning of this
incisive paragraph (again, this is the novel's opening). But how the
writer places and organizes the flow and presentation of his paragraph's
verbal elements clearly affects how the reader apprehends and understands what has been written. Indeed, creating more or less precise
significances, and shadings of significances, in these and in other ways,
is in a sense virtually a definition of what literary style is supposed
to do.

The translator of Flaubert plainly faces enormous challenges, and to
meet those challenges must possess equally large skills.

> We were in class when the head-master came in, followed
> by a "new fellow," not wearing the school uniform, and a
> school servant carrying a large desk. Those who had been

---

3. Ibid., 249.
4. Quoted from Henri Peyre, *French Literary Imagination and Dostoyevsky* (University:
University of Alabama Press, 1975), 54.

asleep woke up, and everyone rose as if just surprised at his work.[5]

In Eleanor Marx Aveling's century-old translation, Flaubert's carefully balanced syntactic movement has quite simply been destroyed. The first sentence is now divided into four approximately equal clauses, none having any greater positional weight than any other; in addition, the parallelism between sentences 1 and 2 has been eliminated. Without for the moment reaching issues of lexicon, it must be noted that the Aveling rendition is in many ways the worst translation of *Madame Bovary* ever to see print: although as we shall see not so untrustworthy in matters strictly lexical, it so distorts Flaubert's style, and thus his stylistic "meaning," that those who know *Madame Bovary* only in this version are apt to seriously misunderstand the book.

> We were in the prep-room when the Head came in, followed by a new boy in "mufti" and a beadle carrying a big desk. The sleepers aroused themselves, and we all stood up, putting on a startled look, as if we had been buried in our work.[6]

As this perhaps even more inept translation indicates, there are plainly many ways to ruin syntactic tracking and obfuscate literary style: this second version (still without any consideration of its lexicon) takes a very different but more or less equally devastating structural path. Mr. May makes the sentences roughly equal in length (25 and then 23 words); he uses only one comma in the first sentence, and three in the second, instead of two in each. And once again there is no reason to expect this translation even to approximate the standards of Flaubert's painstakingly crafted prose.

Penguin, one of our time's most consistent publishers of mediocre translations (almost universally tepid rather than terrible, most usually boring rather than offensive) unfortunately puts out the largest volume of English-language translations. In handling poetry, indeed, Penguin prefers to print prose renderings, thus ensuring that aesthetic and stylistic meanings are not so much distorted as suppressed. In handling prose, Penguin's editors apparently aim at comfortable sameness of style—no sentences too long or too short; as little variety as possible in sentence structure

5. Trans. Eleanor Marx Aveling (New York: Pocket, n.d. [1886]), 3. Rather deceptively labeled "a substantially new translation by Paul De Man," the Aveling translation—now of course in the public domain—was republished by Norton in 1965. Indeed, since it can be printed by anyone without permission or payment of royalties, it is regularly reprinted.

6. Trans. J. Lewis May (New York: Heritage, 1950), 1.

and rhythm; and bland word-choices (monosyllables preferred). Balzac
= Stendhal = Flaubert = Tolstoy = Whoever seems to be the heart of a
determinedly leveling editorial plan.[7] Given the ubiquitousness of Penguin translations, I will of necessity return to this subject later in this
book. For now, and as a faithful exemplar of Penguin's consistently
appalling approach, consider the opening paragraph of *Madame Bovary,*
as translated in 1950 by Alan Russell:

> We were at preparation, when the headmaster came in, fol-
> lowed by a new boy dressed in "civvies" and a school servant
> carrying a big desk. Those who were asleep woke up, and
> everyone got to his feet with an air of being interrupted at
> work.[8]

Without question, Russell's rendering is better attuned to Flaubert's
syntactic movement than either of the truly wretched versions quoted
thus far. But the representation is less than ideal; Flaubert works with a
very fine hand, and his translator cannot ever relax. The first sentence is
roughly parallel in syntactic movement, though the tendency to brisk,
short constructions is already evident: Flaubert's first sentence has, as I
have said, clauses of five and then four words, set off by commas, and
followed by seven- and ten-word phrases linked by "and," while Russell's
first sentence has clauses of four and five words (with only two words of
more than one syllable), also set off by commas, followed however by
phrases of only eight and seven words. The diminution is small, in
absolute terms, but large, both relatively (ten words reduced to seven, for
example, is a 30 percent drop) and stylistically, as we will see still more
clearly when we come to lexical matters. But the second sentence, which
in Flaubert starts with a five-word clause, then moves to a four-word
clause, both set off by commas, and concludes with a five-word phrase, in
Russell's version becomes a six-word clause, set off by a comma, and
concluding with a thirteen-word clause. Again, this is tolerable, all other
things being equal—but all other things, including all other translations,
are in fact not equal.

7. A reviewer—British, as I recall—once observed, wickedly, that the founder of the
Penguin Classics series, E. V. Rieu, in his versions of Homer had discovered that Homer was
in reality Anthony Trollope.

8. Trans. Alan Russell (Harmondsworth: Penguin, 1950), 15. It is worth noting that by
1984, the date of the edition I happen to have in front of me, this translation had been
reprinted no fewer than twenty-seven times. Whether it has been supplemented or replaced
by Geoffrey Wall's new translation (London: Penguin, 1992) is not clear. In any case, the
newer rendering reached me too late for consideration here.

We were studying when the headmaster came in, followed by a new boy, not yet wearing a school uniform, and a monitor carrying a large desk. Those of us who had been sleeping awoke, and we all stood up as if we had been interrupted in our work.[9]

Word counts do not match much differently here, but the pattern of movement does: remove the more or less optional third comma in sentence 1, and add an optional comma after "stood up," in sentence 2, and the syntactic flow becomes distinctly Flaubert-like.

We were in study-hall when the headmaster entered, followed by a new boy not yet in school uniform and by the handyman carrying a large desk. Their arrival disturbed the slumbers of some of us, but we all stood up in our places as though rising from our work.[10]

Again, add optional commas after "study-hall" in sentence 1, and after "our places" in sentence 2, and Flaubert's syntactic movement is very nicely reflected; word count is again only roughly approximated. But as discussion of lexical matters will show, this version, by Francis Steegmuller, is arguably the best translation in print. Lowell Bair's version, finally, is in this passage not far behind:

We were in study hall when the headmaster walked in, followed by a new boy not wearing a school uniform, and by a janitor carrying a large desk. Those who were sleeping awoke, and we all stood up as though interrupting our work.[11]

Indeed, adding the same optional commas, and deleting the equally optional comma after "school uniform," produces very Flaubert-like word-counts of 5-5-10-7 for sentence 1 and 5-4-5 for sentence 2. As I have insisted before, however, words are not identical phenomena in different languages, and translations that nicely track syntactic movement must also be evaluated on other scores, notably lexical choice.

To which we now turn. Aveling starts off as if to handle lexicon as freely as syntactic movement. The meaning of *à l'étude* is to "be studying," or as two of the translators render it, "in study hall." "In class" means something very different; given the powers of teachers in those days, there were not likely to be boys actually sleeping during a class. "In the

9. Trans. Mildred Marmur (New York: Signet, 1964), 27.
10. Trans. Francis Steegmuller (New York: Modern Library, 1957), 3.
11. Trans. Lowell Bair (New York: Bantam, 1959), 1.

prep-room" (May's rendering) is British slang and totally out of place: the rhetorical tone of *à l'étude* is neither slang nor in any way parochial. Alan Russell's version, "at preparation," is rhetorically consistent with the French. I do not know if this is good British usage: G. N. Garmonsway's British dictionary identifies "preparation" with what in the United States is called "homework,"[12] and Garmonsway is reliable. I know nothing of Mr. Russell's literary reputation: if not a mistranslation, this is clearly a limited usage. "We were studying" (Marmur) is dead right, and both "in study-hall" (Steegmuller) and "in study hall" (Bair), though also limited usages (American, that is, rather than British), are in no way mistranslations.

En bourgeois is not a negative construction, but the translator must be allowed some linguistic rope, and the variations on "not yet wearing the school uniform" are unexceptionable. However, May's "in 'mufti' " and Russell's "in 'civvies' " are rhetorically inconsistent with the French, as the embarrassed quotation marks indicate. The fact that Flaubert uses a singular verb form (*se leva*) with *chacun* (each/all of us) need not bind the translator, so that all the versions, singular or plural, are satisfactory, as are the assorted renderings of the preceding phrase (plural in the French), "ceux qui dormaient" ("those who were asleep/slept/were sleeping"), and the various translations of *se réveiller* (to wake up/be roused) and *se leva* (rose/stood up). "Comme surprise dans son travail" ("as if surprised in his [*son* here refers back to *chacun*] work/labors") is also handled freely, but there is not much to choose from, as between and among "as if just surprised at his work" (Aveling), "as if we had been interrupted in our work" (Marmur), "as though rising from our work" (Steegmuller), and "as though interrupting our work" (Bair). "Putting on a startled look, as if we had been buried in our work" (May) and "with an air of being interrupted at work" (Russell) seem both too wordy and too presumptuous in their freedoms.

What lexical analysis indicates, accordingly, is a general failure of correspondence between the ways in which the six translators handle syntactic movement on the one hand and lexical usages on the other. Except for her poor handling of *á l'étude,* Aveling makes some amends for her structural insensitivity by being, on the whole, lexically precise: this comports well with my statement, earlier, that the vast majority of translators are and seem always to have been far more conscious of word meaning than of other aspects of prose translation. May is equally poor on both scores. Russell is somewhat worse in lexical matters, whereas Marmur, Steegmuller, and Bair are more or less equally accomplished in

12. G. N. Garmonsway, ed., *The Penguin English Dictionary* (Harmondsworth: Penguin, 1965), 538b.

each. Translation, like the creation of literature, is an art and not a science, nor do I pretend to have discovered the philosopher's stone: as before, in deciding between and among the last three versions, here, we not only need to use all the assorted tools of measurement available to us but need, equally plainly, not to base the evaluation of a book-length translation on even so pregnant a two-sentence opening paragraph as that Flaubert created for *Madame Bovary*. Would Aveling's translation, examined in more detail, be structurally wayward and lexically secure, as in this first paragraph? Would other differences emerge? Here is the first of two sets of additional evidence, chosen from near the end of chapter 8 of the novel's second part. I give first the French and immediately thereafter, without intervening comment, the six translations, in the same order as before:

> Rodolphe, le dos appuyé contre le calicot de la tente, pensait si fort à Emma, qu'il n'entendait rien. Derrière lui, sur le gazon, des domestiques empilaient des assiettes sales; ses voisins parlaient, il ne leur répondait pas; on lui emplissait son verre, et un silence s'établissait dans sa pensée, malgré les accroissements de la rumeur. Il rêvait à ce qu'elle avait dit et à la forme de ses lèvres; sa figure, comme en un miroir magique, brillait sur la plaque des shakos; les plis de sa robe descendaient le long des murs, et des journées d'amour se déroulaient à l'infini dans les perspectives de l'avenir.

> [*Aveling:*] Rodolphe, leaning against the calico of the tent, was thinking so earnestly of Emma that he heard nothing. Behind him on the grass the servants were piling up the dirty plates, his neighbors were talking; he did not answer them; they filled his glass, and there was silence in his thoughts in spite of the growing noise. He was dreaming of what she had said, of the line of her lips; her face, as in a magic mirror, shone on the plates of the shakos, the folds of her gown fell along the walls, and days of love unrolled before him in the vistas of the future.[13]

> [*May:*] Rodolphe, leaning back against the canvas of the tent, was thinking so deeply of Emma that he heard nothing. Behind him on the grass the servants were piling up the dirty plates; his neighbors spoke, but he did not answer them; they filled up his glass, but silence reigned in his mind, despite the ever-growing clamour. He pondered on what she had said and on the shape of her lips. Her face shone as in a magic mirror in the

13. Trans. Aveling, 161.

badges of the shakos; the folds of her gown hung droopingly on the walls, and days of love stretched out in an endless line down the long vistas of the future.[14]

[*Russell:*] Rodolphe leant back against the side of the marquee, too deep in his thoughts of Emma to hear a thing. On the grass behind him, servants were piling up the dirty plates. His neighbors spoke to him and received no answer. They refilled his glass, but though the hubbub grew around him, all was quiet within his mind. He was thinking of the things she had said, and of the shape of her lips. Her face appeared to him in the cap badges of the militia, shining as in a magic mirror. The pleats of her dress hung down the walls; and days of love unfolded endlessly before him in the long vistas of the future.[15]

[*Marmur:*] Rodolphe, leaning back against the side of the tent, was concentrating so much on Emma that he heard nothing. Behind him, on the lawn, the servants were stacking the dirty dishes; his neighbors addressed him, but he did not answer. His glass was filled and, despite the increasing volume of the sound, in his mind there was silence. He was dreaming about what she had said and the shape of her lips; her face, as in a magic mirror, was shining on the badges of the military caps. The folds of her dress were draping the walls, and days of love unfurled into infinity in the perspective of the future.[16]

[*Steegmuller:*] Rodolphe, his back against the cloth side of the tent, was thinking so much about Emma that he was aware of nothing going on around him. Out on the grass behind him servants were stacking dirty plates; his tablemates spoke to him and he didn't answer; someone kept filling his glass, and his mind was filled with stillness despite the growing noise. He was thinking of the things she had said and of the shape of her lips; her face shone out from the plaques on the shakos as from so many magic mirrors; the folds of her dress hung down the walls; and days of love-making stretched endlessly ahead in the vistas of the future.[17]

14. Trans. May, 150.
15. Trans. Russell, 164.
16. Trans. Marmur, 154.
17. Trans. Steegmuller, 171.

[*Bair:*] Rodolphe, sitting with his back against the cotton tent, was thinking so hard about Emma that he heard nothing. Behind him, on the grass, servants were piling up dirty dishes; the people around him spoke to him but he did not answer; someone kept refilling his glass and there was silence in his mind, despite the growing clamor. He was thinking about the things she had said, and about the shape of her lips; her face shone in the plaque of each shako as in a magic mirror; the folds of her dress hung down the walls, and days of love-making stretched forth endlessly into the future.[18]

The French passage has three sentences. The first is twenty words long and is broken by three commas. The second is thirty-seven words long, divided into three clauses broken by a pair of semicolons, with two commas in the first clause, one in the second, and two in the third. The third and longest sentence, with fifty-four words, once again contains three clauses broken by a pair of semicolons, but in a different rhythm: no commas in the first clause, and one each in the second and third, but with twenty-six words (or roughly half the sentence) in the long final clause.

Without analyzing the six translations in complete detail, we find the following:

Aveling this time tracks syntactic movement well, but does poorly with lexicon: "calico" for *calicot* (used by none of the other versions) is strictly a British usage and distinctly something of a "false friend"; "of the tent" is very much a mechanical *la plume de ma tante* aping of the French structure, unacceptable in any variety of English; *fort* indicates "strength, intensity," not "earnestness"; "piling up" is not as idiomatic, for *empilaient,* as "stacking" (used by Marmur and Steegmuller); "*they* filled his glass" (used by May and Russell) creates pronoun reference problems not present in the French; "built up" or "settled" would be a far stronger, as well as more accurate rendering of *s'établissait* than the limp rendering, "was"; "line" is similarly weak and unevocative for *la forme* (form, shape, appearance); and "the plates of the shakos," also used by Steegmuller and Bair, is truly ludicrous for "la plaque des shakos" ("metal plates at the front of stiff military dress hats").

May uses four sentences instead of three and is generally inadequate both structurally and lexically; he handles *calicot* and *fort* better than Aveling does, but "reigned" for *s'établissait* is archly out of place; "pondered" for *rêvait* ("was dreaming, day-dreaming") is terribly wrong; "the badges of the shakos" (also used by Russell and Marmur) is no better

---

18. Trans. Bair, 131.

than "the plates" (or "the plaques") "of the shakos"; and "hung droopingly" for *descendaient* is totally out of place. (None of the translations picks up on the contrast of Rodolphe's mental "unfolding," *se déroulaient,* of the "folds" [*plis*] of her dress.)

The Penguin translation, by Russell, previously more or less inept both structurally and lexically, chops Flaubert's three flowing sentences into seven itty-bitty ones; nothing could redeem so total a betrayal, and the lexical treatment, here, is once again inadequate: "il ne leur répondait pas" ("he didn't answer them") becomes the indirect and passive "received no answer"; *s'établissait* is as weakly handled here as in Aveling's translation; "thinking" is a pallid rendering of *rêvait;* and "the pleats . . . hung down" for "les plis . . . descendaient" is remarkably feeble.

Marmur, who came off well on the first round, unnecessarily adds two sentences to Flaubert's three, though by carefully avoiding Russell's sparse flatness she does less damage than might otherwise have occurred. Lexically there are some very good touches: "concentrating," "stacking," and "his glass was filled" are good, and "shining on the badges of the *military* caps" (emphasis added) is the best of all the translations in its handling of "la plaque des shakos"; "draping the walls" is ingenious; and "unfurled into infinity" for *se déroulaient* is an extremely sensitive translation. But *parlaient* means "spoke," not "addressed," and "in his mind there was silence" is, again, singularly limp for *un silence s'établissait.*

Steegmuller, who also scored high on round one, tracks the syntactic movement very well indeed; only Bair does as well. There are some splendid lexical touches, especially "thinking so much" for "pensait si fort," "*out* on the grass behind him" (emphasis added), which alone among these translations transmits something of the "turf" meaning of *gazon,* and "shone out" for *brillait.* Steegmuller's sensitivity, too, shines out both structurally and lexically (though "the plaques of the shakos" remains a poor rendering).

Bair comes off second best on this round. Structurally he does well, but lexically he is a bit limp in places, notably with "there was silence in his mind" (compare Steegmuller's "his mind was filled with stillness") and "stretched *forth,*" which is far too wordy for *se déroulaient.*

Here then is the final set of comparative renderings, chosen from near the beginning of the eleventh chapter of the novel's third and last part:

Les affaires d'argent bientôt recommencèrent, M. Lheureux excitant de nouveau son ami Vinçart, et Charles s'engagea pour des sommes exorbitantes; car jamais il ne voulut consentir à laisser vendre le moindre des meubles qui *lui* appartenu. Sa mère en fut exaspérée. Il s'indigna plus fort qu'elle. Il avait changé tout à fait. Elle abandonna la maison.

[*Aveling:*] Money troubles soon began again, Monsieur Lheureux urging on anew his friend Vinçart, and Charles pledged himself for exorbitant sums; for he would never consent to let the smallest of the things that had belonged to *her* be sold. His mother was exasperated with him; he grew even more angry than she did. He had altogether changed. She left the house.[19]

[*May:*] Before long the money troubles began again, Monsieur Lheureux putting his friend Vinçart once more on the war-path, and Charles involved himself in exorbitant liabilities; for he would never agree to part with anything, however trifling, that had belonged to *her.* This enraged his mother. His wrath exceeded hers. He had changed completely. She shook the dust of the place off her feet.[20]

[*Russell:*] Money troubles soon began again, with Lheureux once more egging on his friend Vinçart. Charles bound himself for exorbitant sums; for he would never agree to the sale of the least of *her* possessions. This annoyed his mother. However, his anger vanquished hers. He had altogether changed. She took herself off.[21]

[*Marmur:*] Money troubles soon started again, Lheureux again urging his friend Vinçart on. Charles signed notes for some exorbitant sums since he was determined not to let the least bit of furniture that had belonged to "her" be sold. His mother was furious with him. He grew angrier than she. He had changed completely. She left the house for good.[22]

[*Steegmuller:*] Before long the question of money came up again. Monsieur Lheureux egged on his friend Vinçart as before, and Charles signed notes for enormous sums; he refused absolutely to consider selling the slightest bit of furniture that had belonged to her. His mother fumed; he flew into an even greater rage. He was a completely changed man. She packed up and left.[23]

19. Trans. Aveling, 361.
20. Trans. May, 340.
21. Trans. Russell, 352.
22. Trans. Marmur, 315. Note that this translation divides the novel's third and final part into only ten chapters; there is no explanation for the alteration.
23. Trans. Steegmuller, 386.

[*Bair:*] Money troubles soon began again. Monsieur Lheureux goaded his friend Vinçart as he had done before, and Charles signed notes for exorbitant sums, because he refused to sell any of *her* belongings. His mother was furious with him. His anger was even greater than hers. He had changed completely. She moved out of the house.[24]

The French structure is crystal clear: a long initial sentence broken by, first, two commas and then by a semicolon, is immediately followed by four extremely short sentences. This sharply contrastive syntactic movement closely matches, and of course also expresses, Flaubert's meaning; we tinker with it at our peril (and to Flaubert's disadvantage). The lexicon too is essentially black-and-white—short, simple words of unmistakable significance, for which we should not substitute words meaning anything different.

It is similarly easier to sum up and evaluate what the six translations do here:

Aveling fuses two of the four short sentences (as does Steegmuller); though the long first sentence is retained, the French *car,* immediately after the semicolon, is not syntactically the same as "for" (also used in the other weak translations, May's and Russell's), and the syntactic movement is thus to some extent clogged. Lexically too, this translation is reasonably close to the tone of the French, though "exasperated" for *exaspérée* is both somewhat tepid and also the kind of "false friend" that second- and third-rate translators frequently rely on, and "more angry" is considerably less idiomatic than "angrier." If this rendering scores somewhat higher than Aveling usually does, it remains a tepid translation at best.

May keeps the syntactic movement, though here too "for" does not satisfactorily render *car.* But lexically this is disastrously bad: "the war-path" is terrible; "exorbitant liabilities" is tonally very wrong; "wrath" is not much better; and "shook the dust of the place off her feet" is quite simply incompetent. So too is this translation.

Russell manages, as the Penguin translations so frequently do, to transmit neither the syntactic movement nor the lexicon. The flow of the first sentence is (a) broken and (b) syntactically shifted by the insertion of "with." The four short sentences that end the passage are preserved, but placing "however" before the second of them destroys their blunt movement. "Annoyed" is exceedingly limp, for *exaspérée;* the French says nothing at all about the mother being "vanquished"; and "took herself

24. Trans. Bair, 295.

off" may be suitable British slang, but it does not adequately translate "abandonna la maison" ("forsook/quit/left the house").

Marmur botches the long sweep of the first sentence, not only by breaking it into short elements but also by (a) the monotonous, dulling repetition of "again," where the French carefully uses *recommencèrent* and *de nouveau,* (b) by the wordy and unnecessary "*some* exorbitant sums" (emphasis added), and (c) by the densely agglutinative syntax, words piled heavily one on top of the other. The four short concluding sentences remain, but once again they are not permitted to operate as they do in the original: there is nothing here for them to be contrasted to. To turn to lexicon: *meubles* can of course mean "furniture," but it is clear from the context that here it means "personalty," or "things." Nor do the quotation marks around the word "her" satisfactorily render the effect of the italic emphasis in the original. "She left the house for good" is a fine handling of the blunt last sentence, but it does not sufficiently compensate for the defects that have come before.

Steegmuller, by making two sentences where the original has but one, dims but does not eliminate the sweep of the long first sentence: the new first sentence, having only nine words, is followed by a new second sentence of almost appropriate complexity. "His mother fumed" is lexically deft, as is "he flew into an ever greater rage"; on the other hand, these lexical gains are somewhat offset by the use of a semicolon rather than a period between these two clauses. "She packed up and left" is as fine a rendering, in its way, as Marmur's final sentence. This is on the whole the best translation, in this passage as throughout the book.

Bair also breaks the first sentence, but though the new second sentence is long, its overly balanced three clauses cannot create even a simulacrum of the needed sweep. Again, the four final sentences are all sufficiently short, but they have nothing to contrast with. There are no lexical deficiencies, but structural shortcomings keep the passage from having anything like the meaning of the original.

And what we can conclude from this consideration of six translations of *Madame Bovary* is more or less what we concluded from similar examinations earlier. Syntactic tracking is the key; lexical approximation comes a close second; and success in handling both of these factors largely determines success overall. We cannot of course expect perfection of any translator. (Can we, indeed, legitimately expect perfection of any human performance?) On balance, Steegmuller's is plainly the best of these six versions; Marmur's is next most reliable; then comes Bair's. The first three translations are none of them reliable representations of Flaubert's French original.

Boccaccio's *Decameron* (1352), an early and pioneering prose classic, has over the years suffered a good many humiliations, in part because of its sometimes risqué narratives, in part because to many translators "early" means "primitive, clumsy." Here, as in the rest of the exemplars in this chapter, we will use only one illustrative passage: the point is not fully to evaluate any one translation but to consider the approach to syntactic tracking taken by each. Attention to lexical issues will be intermittent rather than thorough.

Here then is roughly half the long fifth paragraph of the story of Landalfo, told as the fourth tale of the *Decameron*'s second day. Our hero has first been piratically beggared and then shipwrecked:

> Intra li quali il misero Landalfo, ancora che molte volte il dí davanti la morte chiamata avesse, seco eleggendo di volerla piú tosto che di tornare a casa sua povero come si vedea, vedendola presta n'ebbe paura; e, come gli altri, venutagli alle mani una tavola, a quella s'appiccò, se forse Iddio, indugiando egli l'affogare, gli mandasse qualche aiuto allo scampo suo: e a cavallo a quella, come meglio poteva, veggendosi sospinto dal mare e dal vento ora in qua e ora in là, si sostenne infino al chiaro giorno. Il quale venuto, guardandosi egli dattorno, niuna cosa altro che nuvoli e mare vedea, e una cassa la quale sopra l'onde del mare notando, talvolta con grandissima paura di lui gli s'appressava, temendo non quella cassa forse il percotesse per modo che gli noiasse; e sempre che presso glia venia, quanto potea con mano, come che poca forza n'avesse, la lontanava. Ma come che il fatto s'andasse, avvenne che, solutosi subitamente nell'aere un groppo di vento e percosso nel mare, sí grande in questa cassa diede e la cassa nella tavola sopra la quale Landolfo ere, che, riversata, per forza Landolfo lasciatala andò sotto l'onde e ritornò suso notando, piú da paura che da forza aiutato, e vide da sé molto dilungata la tavola: per che, temendo non potere ad essa pervenire, s'appressò alla cassa la quale gli era assai vicina, e sopra il coperchio di quella posto il petto, come meglio poteva, colle braccia la reggeva diritta. E in questa maniera, gittato dal mare ora in qua e ora in là, senza mangiare, sí come colui che non aveva che, e bevendo piú che non avrebbe voluto, senza sapere ove si fosse o vedere altro che mare, dimorò tutto quel giorno e la notte vegnente.

A lot is going on in these four intricately spun sentences; our hero's life is clearly at high risk, and his position is at best extremely precarious. Four sentences spaced out down the page, as these are, by a pair of colons, a pair of semicolons, and thirty-nine commas, must of necessity ebb and flow something like the waves and tides themselves. The translator into English cannot precisely match the incessant movement of the Italian—but he must try to reflect as much of it as he can, and certainly must not destroy it.

> Among them was the unhappy Landolfo. Many times that day he had called upon death and had determined to kill himself rather than return home in such poverty; but when he saw death face to face, he was afraid. He did as the others did, and when a table came to his hands he clutched it, as though God, by delaying his being drowned, had sent him a means of safety. He lay straddled on it as best he could, and, tossed hither and thither by wind and waves, kept himself afloat until daylight. As he gazed around he could see nothing but clouds and sea and a chest he noticed floating on the water near him. With terror he found this chest coming nearer to him, for he was afraid that if the chest hit him he should be drowned. And each time it came very close he thrust it away with his hand as far as his weakness allowed.
>
> Suddenly a blast of wind and a huge wave threw the chest on to Landolfo's table, which upset and plunged him under the waves. He came up again, more through terror than strength, and saw the table already drifting away in the distance. Fearing he could not reach it, he swam to the chest which was close at hand, resting his body on top of it and keeping it upright with his arms, as best he could. All that day and all the next night he was tossed about on the sea in this manner, with nothing to eat and a great deal too much to drink, not knowing where he was, and seeing nothing but the waves.[25]

Instead of four sentences, Aldington uses eleven; instead of thirty-nine commas, he uses eighteen; there are no colons, though the original used two, and there is one semicolon instead of two. Indeed, instead of roughly one-half a paragraph we have two full paragraphs. In short, prose structure and syntactic movement are utterly disregarded: the reader of this translation can have no possible idea of Boccaccio's style, Boccaccio's literary approach, and, inevitably (even though we have said nothing about lexical matters), Boccaccio's full meaning.

25. Trans. Richard Aldington (New York: Doubleday, 1930; reprint, New York: Dell, 1962), 100.

Among them was poor Landolfo, who the day before had indeed wished for death a hundred times, as a fate preferable to returning home a beggar; but now that he saw death close at hand, he changed his mind, and when a plank came his way, he grasped it firmly, in the hope that if he delayed his fate, God would send him some effective help; and riding upon it as well as he could, while the sea and the wind drove him backwards and forwards, he lasted out until the morning. Looking around him by the light of day, he could see nothing but cloud and water, except for a floating box, which drove towards him from time to time, much to his dismay, for he feared that it would dash against him. He kept pushing it away with his hand, though he had little strength left in his body.

But in the end a sudden squall of wind swept down from the sky, and struck the box with such violence that it drove against Landolfo's plank and overturned it, sending him far below the surface; and when he struggled up again, with fear lending strength to his weary limbs, he found that his plank had been carried far away by the waves, so that he doubted whether he could reach it again; and swimming over to the box, which was much nearer, he managed to rest his chest upon it, and held it upright as well as he could with both arms. And in this manner, driven to and fro by the sea, eating nothing because he had no food, and drinking much more than he desired, not knowing where he was nor seeing anything but the waves, he passed the whole of that day and the following night.[26]

This is clearly a good deal closer to the shape and flow of the original. Penman uses five sentences, where Aldington had eleven (and Boccaccio four). He uses twenty-eight commas, where Aldington used eighteen (and Boccaccio thirty-nine); in compensation for the reduced number of commas, however, Penman uses four semicolons, where Aldington uses one (and Boccaccio two). There are no colons. Not only is the prose structure and the syntactic flow closer to the original, so too is the handling of lexicon. Without making a word-for-word comparison, the clearest lexical differences are "plank" for *una tavola* (table, board, plank, slab), in a context where Aldington's "table" is clearly inappropriate, and "box" for *una cassa* (box, trunk, case, coffer), where again Aldington's "chest" is arguably somewhat less accurate. Note too that in Aldington it is Landolfo's "body" that he rests on the *cassa*, where in Penman it

26. Trans. Bruce Penman, in *The Penguin Book of Italian Short Stories,* ed. Guido Waldman (Harmondsworth: Penguin, 1969), 39.

is specifically Landolfo's "chest" that assumes this position; the latter is indeed what the Italian *il petto* (chest, breast, bosom) is intended to signify. And though the Italian author did not have to concern himself with a confusion, or any degree of lexical or rhetorical interference, as between *cassa* and *petto,* the translator into English does have to think about a possible conflict between the homonyms "chest" (box) and "chest" (of the body). It is not surprising (though as we have seen it does not always follow) that a translator who pays attention to one of the most important aspects of his original (syntactic movement) will also pay attention to others (lexicon and rhetoric).

It is both gratifying and, considering how general is the unawareness of syntactic considerations, also surprising that the recent American translation, by Mark Musa and Peter Bondanella, consciously emphasizes this generally underappreciated component of prose translation:

> Some translators feel the need to break Boccaccio's lengthy and complicated period [i.e., Latinate periodic sentences] into as many as four shorter sentences, thus transforming this unique style into something tenser and more conversational. While shorter sentences may be more appealing to the general reader, we feel that great works of literature have earned the right to make certain demands upon their audience. One of the demands Boccaccio makes upon his reader *and* his translator arises precisely from his sometimes extremely complex sentence structure.[27]

Here then is the version produced by these translators:

> Poor Landolfo was among them, and while the day before he had called upon Death to take him, preferring to die rather than return home impoverished as he was now, seeing Death close at hand, he was afraid, and like the others he, too, clung to the first plank that came within reach in the hope that perhaps if he delayed his drowning, God might come to his rescue; he lay straddled on the plank as best he could, and tossed back and forth by the sea and the wind, he held on until daybreak. When he saw the light of day, he looked around him and found nothing but clouds and sea and a chest which floated on the waves, and from time to time, to his great terror, it would drift toward him, for he was afraid that it might hit him and drown him; and every

27. "Translators' Preface," in Giovanni Boccaccio, *The Decameron,* trans. Mark Musa and Peter Bondanella (New York: New American Library, 1982), xxxi–xxxii.

time it got too close to him, as best he could, with his hand and with the little strength he had left, he would push it away. But as luck would have it, suddenly the sea was struck by a strong gust of wind that drove the chest against the plank to which Landolfo was clinging, turning it over and causing Landolfo to lose his grip and sink beneath the waves; thanks more to his fear than his strength, he came up swimming only to see that his plank had floated far off, and so, fearing that he might not be able to reach it, he swam toward the chest, which was closer, and he draped himself over its lid, as best he could, keeping it upright with his arms. And in this fashion, tossed about this way and that by the sea, without a thing to eat and far more to drink than he might have wished, not knowing where he was and seeing nothing but ocean, he floated all that day and the following night.[28]

We find four sentences, an exact match with the Italian; thirty-three commas, which approximate the thirty-nine of the Italian; three semicolons, instead of two; and no colons. There is indeed a general sense of Latinate periodic structures. Why then do we have the sense that Musa and Bondanella's translation is more awkward than Penman's, at times clumsy, even unidiomatic? (It does not help that Musa and Bondanella do not seem fully to understand English punctuation, in particular the use of a *pair* of commas to set off a clause or a phrase, much as a parenthesis or a pair of dashes might do; they frequently use only the first of the pair, which makes for inelegant and sometimes confusing syntactic movement: "thanks more to his fear than his strength, he came up swimming only to see. . . .") Our dissatisfaction stems, alas, from the fact that, rather than tracking syntactic movement—that is, the flow and general shape of Boccaccio's style—they have chosen to quite closely ape the actual syntax of the Italian, a procedure that cannot produce good results in English or indeed in any other language. To illustrate, let me set together, first, the second sentence of the Italian, then a clumsy word-for-word English rendering, and finally the Musa and Bondanella translation:

Il quale [i.e., chiaro giorno] venuto, guardandosi egli dattorno, niuna cosa altro che nuvoli e mare vedea, e una cassa la quale sopra l'onde del mare notando, talvolta con grandissima paura di lui gli s'appressava, temendo non quella cassa forse il percotesse per modo che gli noiasse; e sempre che presso gli venia, quanto potea con mano, come che poca forza n'avesse, la lontanava.

28. Trans. Musa and Bondanella, 83.

The which having come, he looked around, and saw nothing but clouds and sea, and a box which he noted on the waves, which toward him sometimes, with immense fear, [he saw] approaching, afraid that that box might perhaps strike him in such a way that it would bother [hurt] him; and always [each time] when it came near him, as well as he could with his hand, since he did not have much strength [left], he [pushed] it away.

When he saw the light of day, he looked around him and found nothing but clouds and sea and a chest which floated on the waves, and from time to time, to his great terror, it would drift toward him, for he was afraid that it might hit him and drown him; and every time it got too close to him, as best he could, with his hand and with the little strength he had left, he would push it away.

The disastrous and very direct effect of the Italian syntax on the English translation is I think quite obvious. "Every time it got too close to him, as best he could, with his hand and with the little strength he had left, he would push it away" is comprehensible English, but it is not idiomatic, and jars badly. It follows the Italian much too closely for linguistic comfort. So too "from time to time, to his great terror, it would drift toward him, for he was afraid that it might . . . ": indeed, it is not readily apparent, in English, how the syntax gets from "to his great terror, it would drift toward him" to "for he was afraid . . . " That is, "for" suggests a causative link, and of course that link exists in the Italian: "con grandissima paura . . . temendo," but the implied suggestion that the *cassa* approaches him *because* of "his great terror" is distinctly confusing. Comprehensibility at least would have been assured, had the translators said something like "he being afraid," thus preserving the syntactic effect of the participle *temendo.* But these are exactly the kinds of mistakes one is apt to make, in getting so close to the exact forms of the original that the original succeeds in imposing those forms on the translation. I think that what I said of poetic translation, nearly thirty years ago, holds true for all translation: "It may seem paradoxical, but in fact is not, that the poet needs to master the original in order to *leave* it, and that he needs to leave it in order to produce lines which reflect the original and yet are successful poetry in the [new] tongue. To be trapped by the original is far worse than not to have understood it properly."[29] I vividly recall being interrupted by my small daughter, one day when I had been working for

29. Burton Raffel, *The Forked Tongue: A Study of the Translation Process* (The Hague: Mouton, 1971), 59; emphasis added.

some hours, and with intense absorption, at my translation of Rabelais, and finding it hard to speak comprehensibly ordered English. I used English words, because I knew the child did not understand French, but I unconsciously arranged them in French order, even using an essentially meaningless translation of a French idiom—French and not English being the language in which, at that moment, I was thinking. I don't know if my daughter thought I'd gone out of my head, but I do know she did not understand me, and I was obliged to clear away the French clouds and try again. Any speaker of English who has spent time in a country where English is not spoken, and has spoken the other tongue while in that country, will have experienced the linguistic shock of returning home. Even if we have not experienced the problem ourselves, many of us have seen other native speakers of English temporarily tongue-tied, trying only half successfully to fight off foreign linguistic patterns and properly speak the language they grew up with and with which they are not accustomed to having such difficulties.

Older translations of the *Decameron* exhibit their own deficiencies (*all* translations by their very nature exhibit deficiencies), but these are not likely to include either abject surrender to the original or a fondness for brisk, short sentences. Here is an anonymous version, published in 1620:

> ... among whom, distressed Landolpho, desirous to save his life, if possibly it might be, espied a Chest or Coffer before him, ordained (no doubt) to be the meanes of his safety from drowning. Now although the day before, he had wished for death infinite times, rather than to returne home in such wretched poverty; yet, seeing how other men strove for their lives by any helpe, were it never so little, hee tooke advantage of this favour offred him, and the rather in a necessitie so urgent. Keeping fast upon the Coffer so well as he could, and being driven by the winds and waves, one while this way, and anon quite contrary, he made shift for himselfe till day appeared; when looking every way about him, seeing nothing but clouds, the seas and the Coffer, which one while shrunke from under him, and other while supported him, according as the windes and billowes carried it: all that day and night thus he floated up and downe, drinking more than willingly hee would, but almost hunger-starved thorow want of foode.[30]

Charles S. Singleton, perhaps the best-known living American scholar of Renaissance Italian literature, has recently published a revised version

30. *The Decameron,* ed. Edward Hutton (London: David Nutt, 1909), 119.

of the 1886 John Payne translation, dedicated (in words borrowed from T. S. Eliot's dedication of *The Waste Land*), "to John Payne, il miglior fabbro." Here is this translation, which is only very lightly altered from Payne's older version:

> Among the rest the unfortunate Landolfo, although many a time that day he had called for death (choosing rather to die than return home poor as he found himself), seeing it near at hand, was fearful thereof and like the others, laid hold of a plank that came to his hand, so haply, if he put off drowning awhile, God might send him some means of escape.
>
> Bestriding this, he kept himself afloat as best he might, driven hither and thither by the sea and the wind, till daylight, when he looked about him and saw nothing but clouds and sea and a chest floating on the waves, which now and again, to his great fear, drew near him, for he was afraid that it might dash against him in such a way as to injure him; wherefore, as often as it came near him, he pushed it away from him as best he might with his hand, albeit he had little strength for this. But, however it befell, presently there issued a sudden flaw of wind out of the air, and falling on the sea, smote upon the chest and drove it with such violence against Landolfo's plank that it was overturned and he, himself turning loose of it, perforce went under water. However, he struck out and rising, by swimming, to the surface, aided more by fear than by strength, saw the plank far removed from him, wherefore, fearing he might be unable to reach it again, he made for the chest, which was quite near him, and laying himself flat with his breast on the lid of it, kept it upright with his arms as best he might.
>
> In this way, tossed about by the sea now hither and now thither, without eating, as one indeed who had not the where-withal, but drinking more than he could have wished, he remained all that day and the ensuing night without knowing where he was and descrying nought but sea . . . [31]

But can language that was archaic in 1886 speak usefully yet another century and more down the road? Indeed, Singleton seems so unsure of what sort of diction his time requires that, astonishingly, not all the flailing archaisms here stem from Payne. "Himself turning loose of it," for

31. Trans. John Payne, rev. Charles S. Singleton (Berkeley and Los Angeles: University of California Press, 1982), 101.

example, is completely Singleton's responsibility—and a sore one it is. Nor does the contemporary reviser seem troubled by such violently un-English idioms as a "sudden flaw of wind out of the air," though Italian editors themselves are apt to explain that the original of this phrase really means a "scatenatasi improvisamente una raffica" ("sudden gust/squall of wind blew up"). "One . . . who had not the wherewithal" may well be Payne's idea of a sly joke—a suggestion that the almost drowning man cannot afford to buy himself food. But it is not what Boccaccio wrote or intended, and no reviser should have kept it. The fact that this version retains a good deal of the original's syntactic flow (forty commas, for example, in the course of four sentences and a bit over) is thus totally obviated by severe and in my judgment nearly fatal lexical failures. There are indeed many roads to failure, and those that end in success are both few and exceedingly narrow. Verbose archaisms are no more the true path to good translation of the *Decameron* than are short, choppy sentences.

4

More Famous and Infamous Translations
Doña Perfecta, Augustine's Confessions, La Cousine Bette, Illusions Perdues, Germinal, À la recherche du temps perdu

Benito Pérez Galdós is a stylist ranked, in Spain, close behind the universally acknowledged master of Spanish literature, Miguel Cervantes. Galdós's *Doña Perfecta,* published in 1876, begins and ends with remarkably assured and sure-handed prose, flexible, varied, and commanding. Here are the novel's opening and closing paragraphs:

> Cuando el tren mixto descendente número 65 (no es preciso nombrar la linea) se detuvo en la pequeña estación situada entre los kilómetros 171 y 172, casi todos los viajeros de segunda y tercera clase se quedaron durmiendo ó bostezando dentro de los coches, porque el frío penetrante de la madrugada no convidaba á pasear por el desamparado andén. El único viajero de primera que en el tren venía bajó apresuradamente, y dirigiéndose á los empleados, preguntóles si aquél era el apeadero de Villahorrenda. (Este nombre, como otros muchos que después se verán, es propiedad del autor.) . . .
>
> Esto se acabó. Es cuanto por ahora podemos decir de las personas que parecen buenas y no lo son.

It may seem extraordinarily simple-minded, but just as a trained woodsman can follow the path of an animal by studying the purely visual evidence its feet have left behind it, so too the tracker of syntactic movement can trace out a surprising amount simply by following the graphic evidence left on a page. For example, we can see in the first paragraph a longish first sentence (fifty-nine words) slowed in its forward impetus only by two commas and a brief parenthesis. The second sentence is less than half as long (twenty-five words), yet contains the same number of commas. And the third and final sentence, entirely in parentheses, is again only half as long (thirteen words), yet still has two commas. One might guess, without knowing a word of Spanish, that there was pretty clearly a *mind* at work here, and more than likely an *ear* as well. A similar glance at the final paragraph—keeping in mind that closing a book is a very different affair from starting it—would I think confirm that initial impression: there are two sentences, the first only three words long and containing no internal punctuation, the second sixteen words long and also without internal punctuation. In the crudest terms: Galdós here gives us five sentences, no two of which are even remotely like the other. If variety is the spice, not to say the essence, of life, we have here a writer who is profoundly responsive to that dictum.

Spanish novels only a hundred years old are not often available in more than one translation; for *Doña Perfecta* I know of two, published in 1895 and 1960:

> When the down train No. 65—of what line it is unnecessary to say—stopped at the little station between kilometres 171 and 172, almost all the second- and third-class passengers remained in the cars, yawning or asleep, for the penetrating cold of the early morning did not invite to a walk on the unsheltered platform. The only first-class passenger on the train alighted quickly, and addressing a group of the employés asked them if this was the Villahorrenda station. . . .

> Our story is ended. This is all we have to say for the present concerning persons who seem, but are not good.[1]

> When Number 65, the southbound way-train* [*A way-train in Spain is usually a "mixed train," i.e., one that carries both passengers and freight, and stops at all the stations.], stopped at the small station between milestones 171 and 172 (the name of the line is unnecessary) almost all the second- and third-class passengers stayed in their seats, sleeping or yawning, for the

1. Trans. Mary J. Serrano (New York: Harper, 1895), 1, 319.

piercing cold of daybreak did not invite a stroll along the open platform. The solitary first-class passenger hurriedly alighted and, going up to the trainmen, asked them whether this was the Villahorrenda stop. (This name, like many others to appear later, is copyrighted by the author.) . . .

This story is ended. For the moment, it is all we can say concerning people who appear to be good and are not.[2]

Keeping to crude graphic matters, for the moment (and noting, even at that level, that the author's ironic parenthetical remark about his invented place-name—*Villahorrenda* = "ugly town"—has simply disappeared from the older translation), we find the older version making two sentences of the first paragraph, one of fifty-seven words broken by three commas and a parenthetical-like pair of dashes, the other of twenty-five words, broken by one comma. It takes no very sharp or well-informed eye to see that this is in no way an adequate representation of the syntactic flow in Spanish. The final paragraph has, like the original, two sentences, the first much shorter (four words), the second longer (eighteen words) and broken, unlike the original, by a single comma. The syntactic tracking is plainly better here, though not perfect.

The more recent translation starts with a three-sentence paragraph, like the original, the first containing fifty-four words, four commas, and a parenthesis; the second containing twenty-one words and two commas; the third, as in the original enclosed in parentheses, containing thirteen words and two commas. There is also a footnote; once again, I have included it in the text, as it appears above, but have not included its words in any of my counts. Overall sentence-length is quite close to the Spanish; overall number of punctuation markers is somewhat increased. It seems likely that some more or less adequate presentation of Galdós's sentence flow has been reproduced. The concluding paragraph, as in the older translation matching the original's two sentences, contains a four-word sentence and a nineteen-word sentence; the single comma in the latter, unlike that in the older translation, would seem because of its positioning—early rather than late in the sentence—to be less of an interruption of syntactic movement.

We would thus expect (again, this is not guaranteed; just as all contemporary translations are not superior to all older ones, so too all syntactically aware translations are not lexically superior to syntactically blundering ones) the later version to be distinctly better. And it is, not only on

2. Trans. Harriet de Onís (Woodbury, N.Y.: Barron's, 1960), 1, 235.

syntactic grounds, as well as because it is not censored, but also lexically. A "tren mixto descendente" ("a mixed down train") is handled about equally well in both versions: there is loss as well as gain in explaining the full meaning of *mixto* in a footnote, and "down" versus "southbound" is a matter of local usage (British versus American), as is "kilometres" versus "miles." The rather *Don Quijote*-esque comment, that it is not necessary to identify just what line the train was traveling,[3] works equally well in both the positions used by the translations (earlier or later in the sentence), but the more recent version better reflects the suppleness of Galdós's style. (Still better, I suspect, would be a straightforward "you don't need to know the name of the line.") Similarly, "in the cars" for "dentro de los coches" ("inside the coaches/train cars") is just as good British English as "in their seats" is American, and "penetrating cold" for "el frío penetrante" is neither better nor worse translation than "piercing." But "did not invite *to* a walk" (emphasis added) for "no convidaba á pasear" ("was not inviting/conducive to a walk") seems dated rather than merely regional usage; moreover, "stroll" is more accurate than "walk," here. "The unsheltered platform" for "el desamparado andén" ("the abandoned/ deserted [railway] platform") is a good deal less suggestive than "the open platform," though I would have been happier had the translators not wandered from what seems to me Galdós's primary meaning: *desamparado* simply does not mean either "unsheltered" or "open," though the latter at least allows some of the author's intended meaning to sift through. *Único* is better rendered "solitary" than the rather bland older version's "only"; so too "hurriedly alighted" is more responsive to the original's "bajó apresuradamente" ("alighted/got down hurriedly") than the older version's "alighted quickly." "The trainmen" is a very much superior rendering of *los empleados* than the "literal" but awkward "a group of the employés." And of course the totally unwarranted omission of the original's ironic third sentence is damning.

The brief concluding paragraph is clearly marked, in the Spanish text, as a separately printed chapter; the older translation omits this, substituting a simple blank space. This too is unwarranted and damning. There is no compelling lexical difference between the two versions, though "Esto se acabó" is better translated "This story" than "Our story." (Again, I

3. In the book's famous first sentence, the narrator of *Don Quijote* tells us that his story is to begin "en un lugar de la Mancha, de cuyo nombre no quiero acordarme" ("in a place/town in La Mancha, the name of which I don't want to remember/recollect/think about")—though the 1611 *Tesoro de la Lengua Castellana o Española* of Sebastián Covarrubias suggests that in his and Cervantes' day *acordar* had as much to do with polite- ness as with straightforward recollection: see pp. 34 at 53a, 356 at 15a, and especially 837 at 37a. My own translation of the comment is therefore "I won't bother you with its name."

would myself have preferred something like "And that's the end.") But the superior tracking of syntactic movement is quite clearly a valid evaluative and predictive tool, in examining these two translations.

Saint Augustine's *Confessions,* written in Latin, the language from which Spanish, French, Italian, and other languages as well are descended, is of course literary but not overtly fictional. I turn to it now, not only because it allows us to include something from the large and important realm of nonfictional literary prose, and not only because it takes us back fifteen hundred years and within a millennium of the starting point for European prose, but because Latin is structurally so very different from its more modern children and other relatives. That is, in looking at the tracking of syntactic movement in the following passage, we provide ourselves with yet another fairly distant and therefore uniquely valuable touchstone for evaluating this book's basic argument:

> Et anno quidem illo intermissa erant studia mea, dum mihi reducto a Madauris, in qua vicina urbe iam coeperam litteraturae atque oratoriae percipiendae gratia peregrinari, longinquioris apud Carthaginem peregrinationis sumptus praeparabantur, animositate magis quam opibus patris, municipis Thagastensis admodum tenuis. Cui narro haec? Neque enim tibi, Deus meus, sed apud te narro haec generi meo, generi humano, quantulacumque ex particula incidere potest in istas meas litteras. Et ut quid hoc? Ut videlicet ego et quisquis haec legit cogitemus de quam profundo clamandum sit ad te. Et quid propius auribus tuis, si cor confitens et vita ex fide est? (*Confessions,* book 2, chap. 3)

This is not yet medieval Latin, but neither is it Ciceronian: this is Christian Latin, and it is the voice of a preacher. As Dom David Knowles has put it, this "prose is liquid to fluidity, and rhetorical throughout, but it has an intimacy of disclosure and on occasion an iridescence that is new to Latin literature. . . . Cicero was still a model, but the Latin prose of Augustine, for all the sublime effects he could produce, was far looser in texture."[4] Augustine's virtuosity is not hard to see: the longish first sentence (not long for serious Latin prose) has forty-one words and ends with a period; the very short second sentence has three words and ends with a question mark. There are four commas in that longish first sentence; the third, considerably shorter (twenty-three words), also has

4. David Knowles, "Introduction," Saint Augustine, *The City of God,* trans. Henry Bettenson (Harmondsworth: Penguin, 1972), xxxii, xi.

four commas: its movement is extremely different. It too is followed by a four-word query, but after this query we have, first, a taut declarative sentence of only fifteen words, and then yet another query, but this time one of thirteen words, broken by a comma. The syntactic movement is thus, in a sense, composed of three carefully balanced pairs, the first having a longish declarative followed by a short interrogative, the second having a medium-length declarative followed by a short interrogative, and the third having a shortish declarative followed by an interrogative of almost exactly the same length. By contemporary English-language standards, this is a distinctly exotic pattern: it seems no exaggeration to say, with the Jesuit writer, C. C. Martindale, that "never could he rid himself of his African ferocity dominated by his Latin, Roman splendidness: elaborate as may be his phrases, superb, rhythmic, rhyming his style, it was and remained as un-Greek as possible."[5]

Here is a scholarly 1953 translation, published by an official Catholic press and furnished with both a *Nihil Obstat* and an *Imprimatur*:

> My studies were interrupted during that year, when I was brought back from Madaura* [*long explanatory footnote], in which nearby city I had, as a boarding student, already commenced the study of literature and public speaking, and the funds to pay the expenses of a longer stay in Carthage were being assembled, more by means of the ambition than the wealth of my father, who was a far from rich citizen of Tagaste* [*explanatory footnote].
>
> To whom am I telling these things? Not to Thee, O my God; rather, I tell them before Thee to my own kind, to the human race, no matter how few men may happen upon these pages. For what reason? So that I, and whoever reads this, may realize out of what depths one must cry unto Thee.* [*Cf. Ps. 129.1: the famous lines, *De profundis clamavi ad te.*] What is closer to Thy ears than a heart that is penitent and a life founded on faith?[6]

Despite the presence of four footnotes, and despite the modern preference for short paragraphs (so that the original's long first sentence is now a paragraph unto itself), Bourke's translation tracks Augustine's syntactic movement very closely: six sentences, in three pairs, the first of each pair declarative and in declining order of size, the second of each pair

5. C. C. Martindale, S.J., "A Sketch of the Life and Character of St. Augustine," in *Saint Augustine,* ed. M. C. D'Arcy, S.J. (New York: Sheed & Ward, 1930; reprint, New York: Meridian, 1957), 88.

6. Trans. Vernon J. Bourke (Washington, D.C.: Catholic University of America Press, 1953), 36.

interrogative, the first two short, the third and final interrogative roughly the length of the declarative that precedes it. The semicolon near the start of the second declarative sentence, however, somewhat breaks the syntactic flow. There are also seven commas in the first paragraph, six in the second; however, English is a more expansive language than Latin, almost invariably requiring more words to say the same thing, and when there are more sheep so too must there be more sheep dogs. All in all, even without reaching lexical issues, we would expect Bourke's to closely reflect his original on that score too.

Here is Rex Warner's modernizing translation (published in 1963, and with an introduction by Bourke):

> In this year there was a break in my studies. I came back home from Madaura, the nearby city to which I had gone to learn the beginnings of literature and rhetoric, and now money was being provided for me to go further afield, to Carthage. This was rather because my father had big ideas than because he was rich. He was only a poor citizen of Tagaste. But to whom am I relating this? Not to you, my God. But I am telling these things in your presence to my own kind, to that portion of mankind, however small it may be, which may chance to read these writings of mine. And my object in doing so is simply this: that both I myself and whoever reads what I have written may think *out of what depths we are to cry unto Thee.* For nothing comes nearer to your ears than a confessing heart and a life of faith.[7]

There have been many Englishings of Augustine's *Confessions.* But if what we are seeking is contrastive approaches to the tracking of syntactic movement, it would be hard to find two more sharply divergent versions. Warner has nine sentences, instead of six, and there is quite simply no trace left of the original's pattern of statements and questions. Indeed, there is only one interrogative sentence in Warner's translation of the passage; one of the question marks has been replaced by a colon. There are no footnotes (though there is a ten-word sequence in italics), but the "modernization" here is so intense that although the word count of the two Englishings is almost identical (150 in Warner, 156 in Bourke), short sentences in Warner are matched by a profusion of short words—120 monosyllables, or 80 percent of the total word count, whereas Bourke has only 106 monosyllables, or 68 percent of the word count. The original is necessarily more polysyllabic, Latin being a heavily declined language: predictably,

7. Trans. Rex Warner (New York: Mentor, 1963), 42.

Augustine uses only 98 words, 30 (or barely 31 percent) of which are monosyllables. It would be virtually impossible to match those figures in an English version, but a translation featuring 68 percent monosyllables is plainly a great deal closer to the original than one with 80 percent.

To the extent that tracking syntactic movement is an evaluative and predictive tool, reflecting in a general way a translator's commitment to his original author, we should here expect that, lexically, Bourke will be a good deal closer. Warner starts with active rather than, as in the Latin, passive voice; Bourke preserves even this facet of the original. But though Warner's "a break" is lexically accurate for *intermissa erant* ("were interrupted/broken off"), it is, if not quite slang, certainly colloquial and thus rhetorically, tonally far less accurate than Bourke's "were interrupted." Augustine tells us that he was *reducto* ("brought back") from Madaura, and Bourke so translates; Warner's preference for emphatic modernism leads him to translate "I came back home," which is importantly different. A twentieth-century student makes many if not most of his own decisions; a fourth-century student does not. Augustine tells us that he had been in Madaura, in Bourke's rendering of "percipiendae gratia peregrinari" ("as a boarding student"), but Warner simply omits this information. Warner's "big ideas," for "animositate magis quam opibus patris" ("more from my father's striving than from his wealth"), is strictly slang, and far less satisfactory than Bourke's "more by means of the ambition than the wealth of my father." Warner is also capable of swinging abruptly in the opposite direction, turning *narro* ("tell, report, narrate") into the suddenly quite formal "relating," which Bourke straightforwardly translates as "telling." "Et ut quid hoc?" ("And why?") is similarly rendered by Bourke, "For what reason?" But Warner quite transforms the simple query into the elaborate "And my object in doing so ... " "Et quisquis haec legit" ("And whoever reads this") is similarly rendered by Bourke "and whoever reads this," while Warner translates "and whoever reads what I have written." The difference is not immense; however, it seems distinctly significant: Augustine knows how to be expansive, but he also relishes pithiness. Bourke allows him to have it; Warner does not. Nor is Warner's "a confessing heart" anything like as satisfactory, in a Christian context, for the original's *cor confitens* ("an admitting/acknowledging/confessing heart"), as Bourke's "a heart that is penitent." Bourke is not so graceful a stylist as Warner, and "a heart that is penitent" is not as harmonious as "a confessing heart." Granted. But Bourke's rendering is not awkward—and it comes, I think, a good deal closer to what Augustine wanted to say. Finally, Augustine speaks of "et vida ex fide est" ("and a life [coming] from within faith"). Warner translates, smoothly, "and a life of faith," but once more Bourke's translation is far more sensitive to what Augustine means: "a life founded on faith."

Warner's translation, in short, gives us neither the shape and movement of Augustine's mind nor the true flavor of his words. Bourke's
translation is plainer than the original, sturdy and clear but not in any way
resplendent: to that extent Warner's translation may be judged both more
accessible and, in a certain sense, more representative of the *degree* of
Augustine's achievement. But for the true *nature* of that achievement, go
to Bourke—or even to some flawed but readable nineteenth-century
version, such as Pilkington's:

> And for that year my studies were intermitted, while after my
> return from Madaura (a neighboring city, whither I had begun to
> go in order to learn grammar and rhetoric), the expenses for a
> further residence at Carthage were provided for me; and that was
> rather by the determination than the means of my father, who
> was but a poor freeman of Thagaste. To whom do I narrate this?
> Not unto Thee, my God; but before Thee unto my own kind,
> even to that small part of the human race who may chance to
> light upon these my writings. And to what end? That I and all
> who read the same may reflect out of what depths we are to cry
> unto Thee. For what cometh nearer to Thine ears than a confessing
> heart and a life of faith?[8]

I do not think this translation superior to Bourke's, though it is more
graceful. I do think it vastly superior to Warner's—as are most translations,
frankly, regardless of age or provenance, for Warner's overriding concern
is to be palatable rather than to satisfactorily represent his author. Let me
present, without analyzing, two additional translations in testimony to
that fact; the first is from the nineteenth century, the second dates from
1943:

> For that year were my studies intermitted: whilst after my return
> from Madaura* [*long explanatory footnote] (a neighbor city,
> whither I had journeyed to learn grammar and rhetoric), the
> expenses for a further journey to Carthage were being provided
> for me; and that, rather by the resolution than the means of my
> father, who was but a poor freeman of Thagaste. To whom tell I
> this? not to Thee, my God; but before Thee to mine own kind,
> even to that small portion of mankind as may light upon these
> writings of mine. And to what purpose? that whosoever reads
> this, may think out of what depths we are to cry unto Thee. For

8. Trans. J. G. Pilkington (1876; reprint, New York: Liveright, 1943), 29–30.

what is nearer to Thine ears than a confessing heart, and a life of faith?[9]

In that year my studies were interrupted. I had come back from Madaura, a neighboring city to which I had been sent to study grammar and rhetoric, and the money was being got together for the longer journey to Carthage, where I was to go because my father was set upon it—not that he was rich, for he was only a poor citizen of Tagaste. But to whom am I telling this? Not to Thee, O My God, but in Thy presence I am telling it to my own kind, to the race of men, or rather to that small part of the human race that may come upon these writings. And to what purpose do I tell it? Simply that I and any other who may read may realise out of what depths we must cry to Thee. For nothing is more surely heard by Thee than a heart that confesses Thee and a life in Thy faith.[10]

But I cannot leave Augustine's *Confessions* without at least a rapid glance at the famous passage describing his arrival in Carthage (book 3, chap. 1):

Veni Carthaginem et circumstrepebat me undique sartago flagitiosorum amorum. Nondum amabam et amare amabam et secritore indigentia oderam me minus indigentum. Quaerebam quod amarem, amans amare, et oderam securitatem et viam sine muscipulis, quoniam fames mihi erat intus ab interiore cibo, te ipso, Deus meus, et ea fame non esuriebam, sed eram sine desiderio alimentorum incorruptibilium, non quia plenus eis eram, sed quo inanior eo fastidiosior. Ed ideo non valebat anima mea . . .

To Carthage I came, and a hissing cauldron* ['long explanatory footnote] of shameful loves seethed around me on all sides. I was not in love, yet I loved to love and, in the hidden depths of unsated desire, I hated myself for my partial lack of desire. I sought some object that I might love, loving the very act of love; I hated peace of mind and a path unbeset by pitfalls* ['short footnote]. For, though I was hungry within me with the lack of that inner food which is Thyself, my God, I experienced no longing as a result of that hunger. Rather, I lacked the desire for

9. Trans. Edward B. Pusey (ca. 1836; reprint, New York: Carlton House, 1949), 26.
10. Trans. F. J. Sheed (New York: Sheed & Ward, 1943), 29.

incorruptible nourishment, not because I was filled with it, but, the more empty I was, the greater my loathing became. And that is why my soul was unhealthy . . . [11]

I came to Carthage, and all around me in my ears were the sizzling and frying of unholy loves. I was not yet in love, but I loved the idea of love, and from a hidden want I hated myself for not wanting more. Being in love with love I looked for something to love; I hated security and a path without snares. I was starved inside me for inner food (for you yourself, my God), yet this starvation did not make me hungry. I had no desire for the food that is incorruptible, and this was not because I was filled with it; no, the emptier I was, the more my stomach turned against it. And for this reason my soul was in poor health . . . [12]

The Latin has two short, emphatic sentences, followed by a long and intricate one; I have truncated the next sentence, giving only the first few words. This time Bourke uses one shorter sentence, followed by four sentences of medium length, while Warner too uses five sentences, all except the last, which is somewhat longer, of approximately the same length. Bourke is perhaps a bit closer to the Latin, but in this passage there is not much difference in the degree of syntactic tracking—and, indeed, this is, in Latin, a passage of verbal rather than structural/logical fireworks. Still, the syntactic blandness of Warner's "I came to Carthage" compares unfavorably to the stern drama of Bourke's "To Carthage I came," and indeed throughout this key passage there is a wordiness in Warner's translation that undercuts Augustine's starkness. "Nondum amabam et amare amabam" ("I was not yet in love and what I loved was love") is far better rendered as "I was not in love, yet I loved to love" (Bourke) than as "I was not yet in love, but I loved the idea of love" (Warner). There is a different kind of blandness too in Warner's handling of "Quaerebam quod amarem, amans amare" ("I looked for something to love, loving to love"): "Being in love with love I looked for something to love." Bourke is somewhat too wordy, here, but he at least conveys some of the dignity and pathos of the original: "I sought some object that I might love, loving the very act of love." It is Warner's structural inversion (placing "amans amare" before rather than after "quaerebam quod amarem") that lowers the intensity of his translation, just as it is Bourke's respect for the movement of Augustine's mind across the printed page that gives his translation of this passage what superiority

11. Trans. Bourke, 49.
12. Trans. Warner, 52.

it has. And it is indeed that same "respect" which, in the final analysis, conclusively raises his translation over Warner's.

Passages from two Balzac novels, and one by Zola, will bring us almost to the end of this long chapter. Nineteenth-century French novels being an important part of Penguin's list, when that publisher makes a conscious attempt to reissue "classic" books, we have the opportunity to examine still more translations from the Penguin series. (*Gargantua and Pantagruel* and *Don Quijote,* discussion of which will comprise the second half of this book, are also represented in the Penguin series, and will round out my examination thereof.)

La Cousine Bette (1846), remarks one its most recent editors, is "un des chefs-d'oeuvre les moins discutés de Balzac, son influence sur l'évolution du roman français a été considérable, les naturalistes entre autres l'ayant considéré comme une modèle"[13] ("one of Balzac's least-discussed masterpieces, its influence on the development of the French novel having been considerable, the Naturalists [among others] having taken it as a model"). It is not only critically more or less ignored, especially outside France, but in English translation even its very title is commonly misrepresented. Bette is a two-syllable word in French, with the second syllable a weak *schwa* (like the vowel in the second syllable of "mother"), and *cousine* is unmistakably the feminine form of "cousin." The usual English translation is however *Cousin Bette,* where "cousin" is a word without gender, and "Bette," not strictly an English-language name at all, is likely to be pronounced either "bet" or "Betty." But "Betty" in English is touched with diminutive and colloquial flavors, as *Bette* in French is not. *Cousin Bette* is thus something of a linguistic monstrosity; it is likely to be meaningful only to those who are familiar both with the French language and with the title in that language. These are not, I'm afraid, the people for whom the translation is meant, nor are they the people likely to read it. A translator must therefore either reproduce unchanged the French title, *La Cousine Bette,* or devise some truly effective approximation—or else endeavor, as translators are frequently required to do, to invent a new and totally different title for the book's appearance in a new language. (See for example the discussion of Proust's *À la recherche du temps perdu,* later in this chapter.)

Balzac is a distinctive and very focused, if not a great, stylist: one knows his voice and has little trouble identifying his hand at work in such passages as the following, a very typical disquisition on the nature of women, here representing the feelings and state of mind of Adeline, Baroness Hulot:

13. Roger Pierrot, ed., Honoré de Balzac, *La Cousine Bette* (Paris: Livre de Poche, 1984), 7.

> Elle aurait bien voulu que le baron la prît pour sa confidante; mais elle n'avait jamais osé lui donner à entendre qu'elle connaissait ses fredaines, par respect pour lui. Ces excès de délicatesse ne se rencontrent que chez ces belles filles du peuple qui savent recevoir des coups sans en rendre; elles ont dans les veines des restes du sang des premiers martyrs. Les filles bien nées, étant les égales de leur maris, éprouvent le besoin de les tourmenter, et de marquer, comme on marque les points au billard, leurs tolérances par des mots piquants, dans un esprit de vengeance diabolique, et pour s'assurer, soit une supériorité, soit un droit de revanche.[14]

Balzac employs two medium-length sentences, each of which more or less turns on a semicolon, followed by a long sentence that in typical Balzac fashion marches from one end of a subject to another, spinning relentlessly from comma to comma—nine in all, though there is only one comma in the two medium-length sentences. The apparently calm surrounding of subjects, in a prose of remarkably detailed nervousness, giving an effect at the same time both stately and agitated, seems to me perhaps the dominant quality of Balzac's style generally and of this passage in particular. The translator neglects or distorts it at his or her peril.

> She would very much have liked the Baron to confide in her; but she had never dared to let him know that she knew of his escapades, out of respect for him. Such excessive delicacy is found only in girls of noble character sprung from the people, who know how to take blows without returning them. In their veins flows the blood of the early martyrs. Well-born girls, as their husbands' equals, feel a need to bait their husbands, to score off them as in a game of billiards, to make up for their acts of tolerance by biting remarks, in a spirit of revengeful spite and in order to assure themselves either of their own superiority or of their right to have their revenge.[15]

This plodding, largely tone-deaf prose belongs, alas, to the translation published by Penguin. Superficially not too remarkably distant from the original—four sentences instead of three, and with only one semicolon—this translation in fact frequently tracks French word

14. *La Cousine Bette,* 44.
15. Trans. Marion Ayton Crawford (Harmondsworth: Penguin, 1965), 35.

order without understanding either French or English syntactic movement. Essentially devoid of style, these four sentences do not so much
march across a subject as agglutinate on top of it. I will make this clearer
in a moment; first, here is our other translation, very recently published:

> She would have liked the Baron to confide in her, but out
> of respect for him she had never dared hint that she knew of
> his goings-on. This excessive delicacy is only to be found
> amongst those beautiful daughters of the people who know
> how to receive blows without returning any. The blood of the
> first martyrs flows in their veins. Well-born girls, being their
> husbands' equals, feel the need to torment them and to mark
> their acts of tolerance with biting words, as one marks up the
> score at billiards, in a diabolical spirit of vengeance and to
> assure themselves either of their own superiority or of a right to
> revenge.[16]

This is not so stiffly tied to French word order; the positioning of "out
of respect for him" takes on an English rather than a French coloration.
But it does not sound much like Balzac's prose: again, there are four
sentences, but no semicolons at all; indeed, the long final sentence is not,
relatively speaking, so long, and is broken by four rather than by nine
commas. (The Penguin version has five.) The thoughtful, careful, slow
accretion of ideas and explanations in Balzac has become blandly sequen-
tial and not terribly effective assertion—and since lexical matters are
important in examining both these translations, let me quickly move to
that aspect of things.

The Penguin translation is, bluntly, bowdlerized. "Ces belles filles du
peuple" ("those beautiful girls [born of] the people/common folk")
becomes, God knows how, "girls of noble character." That is, Balzac's
emphasis on physical beauty is redirected, totally without warrant, toward
more spiritual matters. (Such bowdlerization is excruciatingly frequent
both in Rabelais and in Cervantes, as I will show in Part 2.) The Oxford
version far more accurately translates "those beautiful daughters of the
people." And in the Penguin rendition the tart nastinesses of "well-born
girls," which Balzac tells us are spoken "dans un esprit de vengeance
diabolique" ("in a spirit of diabolical vengeance"), are toned down to "a
spirit of revengeful spite." Once more, the Oxford version gets it right:
"in a diabolical spirit of vengeance." But neither translation does justice
to the baroness's strong desire to have her husband "la prît pour sa

16. Trans. Sylvia Raphael (New York: Oxford University Press, 1992), 30.

confidante" ("take her for/as his confidante"); both tone this down to a rather bland "To confide in her." It is not at all the same thing. "Escapades" (Penguin) is satisfactory for *fredaines* (pranks, escapades); the lame rendering "goings-on" (Oxford) is much less satisfactory. The Penguin translation better handles the French *en* construction (*sans en rendre*), with its "Take blows without returning them," than does the Oxford with the clumsy, unidiomatic "receive blows without returning any."

The original's long final sentence shows, however, the fundamental difference between the two translations. Balzac's well-born ladies feel the need to *tourmenter* ("torment, torture, harass") their husbands. In the Penguin rendering this is a bland need to "bait"; in the Oxford it is, correctly, "torment." The similar need to *marquer* ("mark [as one marks a shirt], record, show") their *tolérances* ("tolerance, sufferance") becomes, in the Penguin translation, "to score off" their husbands, "to make up for their acts of tolerance." The original says nothing of the kind. Again, the Oxford version more correctly, albeit not entirely satisfactorily, translates "to mark their acts of tolerance." These well-born ladies do this, says Balzac, carefully repeating the operant verb, "comme on marque les points au billard" ("as one marks points in billiards"). The Penguin softens this to "as in a game of billiards"; the Oxford a bit haltingly but far more trustworthily translates "as one marks up the score at billiards." The Penguin version does however better handle, though not entirely satisfactorily, the *soit . . . soit* (whether/either *this* or *that*) construction at the end of the passage. "Either of their own superiority or of their right to have their revenge" is preferable to "either of their own superiority or of a right of revenge." The French *droit* ("privilege, law, right") requires some bolstering when it is turned into the much weaker English "right."

Plainly, neither version does justice to Balzac on either syntactic or lexical issues, but on both scores the Oxford rendering is at least consistently better. This is to damn with faint praise, to be sure—but to damn a translation is in my opinion better than to permit a translation to damn Balzac.

Illusions Perdues, the three parts of which were published in 1837, 1839, and 1843, is one of the longest of Balzac's novels (though one might perhaps argue that all his novels taken together are no more than one enormously large novel). And it has a long sequel. We will do well to confine ourselves here to the novel's very first paragraph; Balzac has thoughtfully written it in what could almost be considered a parody of his style:

> A l'époque où commence cette histoire, la presse de Stanhope et
> les rouleaux à distribuer l'encre ne fonctionnaient pas encore

dans les petites imprimeries de province. Malgré la spécialité qui la met en rapport avec la typographie parisienne, Angoulême se servait toujours des presses en bois, auxquelles la langue est redevable du mot "faire gémir la presse", maintenant sans application. L'imprimerie arriérée y employait encore des *balles* en cuir frottées d'encre, avec lesquelles l'un des pressiers tamponnait les caractères. Le plateau mobile où se place la *forme* pleine des lettres sur laquelle s'applique la feuille de papier était encors en pierre et justifait son nom de *marbre*. Les dévorantes presses mécaniques ont aujourd'hui si bien fait oublier ce mécanisme, auquel nous devons, malgré ses imperfections, les beaux livres des Elzevier, des Plantin, des Alde et des Didot, qu'il est nécessaire de mentionner les vieux outils auxquels Jérôme-Nicolas Séchard portait une superstitieuse affection, car ils jouent leur rôle dans cette grande petite histoire.

There are five torrentially minute sentences, the last (as so often in Balzac) the longest, piled up with the aid of seven commas. Sentences 1 and 3 have one comma each, sentence 2 has three, and sentence 4 has none. There are no semicolons, no colons, no parentheses. Balzac's grand passion for everything that interests him, whether small or large, fairly pours out at us; indeed, he almost sums up his approach with the final phrase, "cette grande petite histoire" ("this great/grand little history/story/tale"). The translator's task is thus to hold one part of the novel firmly to the ground, while letting the other part soar.

At the time when this story opens, the Stanhope press and the ink-distributing roller had not yet come into use in small provincial printing-houses; and, not withstanding its paper industry, that linked Angoulême so closely with Paris printing, wooden presses—of the kind to which the figure of speech "to make the press groan" was literally applicable—were still in use in that town. Old-fashioned printing-houses were still using leather ink-balls, with which the printers used to ink the type by hand. The movable tables for the formes of type, set ready for the sheets of paper to be applied, were still made of stone and justly called *marbles*. The rapid spread of machine presses has swept away all this obsolete gear to which, for all its imperfections, we owe the beautiful books printed by Elzevir, Plantin, Aldus, Didot, and the rest; so that some description is necessary of the old tools to which Jérôme-Nicolas Séchard was almost superstitiously attached, for they play a part in this great story of small things.[17]

Raine (a well-known British poet) plainly scorns the temptation to chop long sentences into little ones: she uses four sentences where, indeed, Balzac uses five, linking the original's first and second sentences with a semicolon (and using yet another semicolon in the long final sentence), but falling back on a parenthetical insertion to help clarify what is most directly relevant and what is, in fact, parenthetical. The general march of the prose in this translation very closely follows that of the original: Raine's second sentence (Balzac's third) is a particularly exact reflection of the turn of Balzac's style (and of his mind). Without for the moment getting to lexical issues, it is also clear that Raine does extremely well by "cette grande petite histoire": "this great story of small things" seems to me brilliantly right.

> At the time when this story begins, the Stanhope press and inking-cylinders were not yet in use in small provincial printing-offices. Angoulême, although its paper-making industry kept it in contact with Parisian typography, was still using those wooden presses from which the now obsolete metaphor "making the presses groan" originated. Printing there was so much behind the times that the pressmen still used leather balls smeared with ink to dab on the characters. The "follower" holding the letter-filled "forme" to which the paper is applied was still made of marble and so justified its name "imposing stone." The ravenous machines of our time have so completely superseded this mechanism—to which, despite its imperfections, we owe the fine books produced by the Elzevirs, the Plantins, the Aldi and the Didots—that it is necessary to mention these antiquated tools which Jérôme-Nicolas Séchard held in superstitious affection; they have their part to play in this great and trivial story.[18]

Hunt's Penguin translation, like Balzac's original, uses five sentences, and again very closely tracks the movement of the original French. Nor is Hunt's style either stiff or awkward. Plainly, no crude examination of syntactic tracking will be of much use; we must move at once to lexical issues.

Balzac has his story *commence* (begin); Raine has it "open," Hunt has it "begin," and the Penguin version is thus closer to the French.

17. Trans. Kathleen Raine (London: John Lehmann, 1951; reprint, New York: Modern Library, 1985), 17.
18. Trans. Herbert J. Hunt (Harmondsworth: Penguin, 1971), 3.

But "inking-cylinders" (Hunt) is an unnecessarily obscure way of translating "rouleaux à distribuer l'encre" ("rollers for distributing ink"). Raine's "ink-distributing roller" is both clearer and at the same time more accurate. So too, Raine sensitively realizes that, more than a century later and in a different land, Balzac's second sentence seems rather jarringly abrupt, so she softens the impact and clarifies the sense by joining it, via a semicolon, to the first sentence. Both translations explain the "spécialité qui la [i.e., Angoulême] met en rapport avec la typographie parisienne" ("the speciality that puts/places it [Angoulême] in connection/relation with Parisian printing-works"). But Raine, by shunning the etymological link of English "typography" and French *typographie,* manages to keep things clearer; her intensifier, "so closely," is to be sure a freedom, but not a gross one. Neither translation gives a close reading of the groaning wooden presses. "Old-fashioned" (Raine) for *arriérée* ("fallen behind") is more idiomatic than the clumsy "so much behind the times" (Hunt). So too "leather ink-balls" (Raine) allows the translator not to be trapped in the awkward and very wordy "leather balls smeared with ink" (Hunt), just as "to ink the type by hand" (Raine) saves the translator from the curious and somewhat ambiguous "to dab on the characters" (Hunt). What "characters"? The other printers? Or the actual letters? *Frotter* can of course mean "dab," but since it also means "to ink up," when used in the context of a printing press, that is the usage called for. *Pressiers* is as accurately rendered "pressmen" (Hunt) as "printers" (Raine), with "pressmen" being perhaps the more precise. "The 'follower' holding the letter-filled 'forme' " is almost desperately confusing, as well as not reflective of the French; "le plateau mobile où se place la 'forme' pleine de lettres" ("the moving/movable tray on which one places the 'form' full of letters/type") is much more satisfactorily rendered "movable tables for the formes of type" (Raine). "Imposing-stone" (Hunt) for "plateau ... en pierre" ("stone ... tray") is quite simply ghastly; "marbles" (Raine) is hardly ideal, but just as plainly is far more palatable. "The rapid spread of machine presses" (Raine) for "les dévorantes presses mécaniques" ("devouring mechanical presses") is, however, not satisfactory; "the ravenous machines of our times" (Hunt), though also not ideal, is somewhat better. "Fine books" (Hunt) for "beaux livres" (beautiful books) is not as good as "beautiful books" (Raine). We have already seen how well Raine handles the very important final phrase: Hunt's "this great and trivial story" makes for a sorry comparison.

The net judgment plainly favors Raine's translation; again, given that both translators adequately if somewhat imperfectly track syntactic flow, no evaluation can be made simply on that basis. As I have said, a useful but inherently gross tool cannot be used in all circumstances and, just as important, cannot be used as though it were capable of making fine distinctions. What can be said is that if it does *not* offer close tracking of syntactic movement a translation is extremely likely to be unsatisfactory; if however it *does* offer close tracking of syntactic movement it can, if it handles lexical matters equally well (or better), succeed in being a truly useful replication of the original. Whether or not a translation offers close tracking of syntactic movement, accordingly, is more likely to be a *sine qua non* than a decisive evaluative or predictive tool. I have no adequate data base to work from, but—as an impressionistic judgment, based on fairly extensive experience—I suspect that, more often than not, a prose translation that features close tracking of syntactic movement will also feature sensitive handling of lexicon. But translation is an art, not a science, and there are no guarantees.

Zola's *Germinal* (the three translations I shall compare all use the French title, unchanged) is too familiar a book to need any introduction. Powerfully, at times harrowingly written, it is broodingly erotic; it is also drivingly romantic and fiercely polarized. Let us look, not at its beginning, but at its final paragraph:

> Et, sous les pieds, les coups profonds, les coups obstinés des rivelaines continuaient. Les camarades étaient tous là, il les entendait le suivre à chaque enjambée. N'était-ce pas la Maheude, sous cette pièce de betteraves, l'échine cassée, dont le souffle montait si rauque, accompagné par le ronflement du ventilateur? À gauche, à droite, plus loin, il croyait en reconnaître d'autres, sous les blés, les haies vives, les jeunes arbres. Maintenant, en plein ciel, le soleil d'avril rayonnait dans sa gloire, échauffant la terre qui enfantait. Du flanc nourricier jaillissait la vie, les bourgeons crevaient en feuilles vertes, les champs tressaillaient de la pousée des herbes. De toutes parts, des graines se gonflaient, s'allongeaient, gerçaient la plaine, travaillées d'un besoin de chaleur et de lumière. Un débordement de sève coulait avec des voix chuchotantes, le bruit des germes s'épandait en un grand baiser. Encore, encore, de plus en plus distinctement, comme s'ils se fussent rapprochés du sol, les camarades tapaient. Aux rayons enflammés de l'astre, par cette matinée de jeunesse, c'était de cette rumeur que la campagne était grosse. Des hommes poussaient, une armée noire, vengeresse, qui germait lentement dans les sillons, grandissant pour les récoltes du siècle futur, et dont la germination allait faire bientôt éclater la terre.

This passage is not built on any stark alternation of long and short sentences, or of declaratives and interrogatives. Its eleven sentences are of reasonably uniform length, the last being, with rhetorical appropriateness, a touch the longest. There are ten declaratives; only the third sentence is interrogative, the inwardly directed question helping to establish a thoughtful, quasi-introspective tone. There are only commas and periods: no parentheses or parenthetical alternatives, no semicolons, no colons. There are thirty-five commas in all; every sentence has at least one, nor does the last and slightly the longest sentence contain the largest number of commas. The sequence (it cannot truly be called a pattern) is as follows; the single interrogative is marked by italics:

3
1
4
6
3
2
4
1
4
2
5

Zola's rhetoric, clearly, is neither classically based nor regulated by any externally derived schema. His prose unwinds by its own rules, and at its own pace—but as the presence of internal punctuation in every sentence demonstrates, it most definitely unwinds. The complete absence of short sentences is the farthest thing from accidental: Zola has been accused of trying to knock his readers over the head, but I suspect he is more often trying to drown them. This final paragraph of *Germinal* moves neither like a battering ram nor a hurricane but like a flood. The most basic forces of Nature itself, according to Zola, are impelling every powerful movement. And the translator must capture that surging power, that tidal-wave-like intensity, on which Zola's fervent, sometimes overheated lexicon displays itself like the passionate embers of some consciously glowing fire.

> And beneath his feet the heavy, stubborn hammering of the picks was still going on. His comrades were all there—he could hear them follow his every stride. Wasn't that La Maheude under the beet field, her back breaking, her harsh breathing rising in time with the rumble of the ventilator? To the left, to the right, farther

along, he thought he could recognize the others, under the wheat fields, the hedges, the young trees. Now the April sun was high in the sky, blazing gloriously, warming the teeming earth. Life was springing from her nourishing flank, buds were bursting into green leaves, fields were trembling under the push of the grass. On all sides seeds were swelling and stretching, thrusting through the plain in search of warmth and light. There was a whispering rush of overflowing sap, the sound of seeds spread in a great kiss. Again, again, more and more distinctly, as if they too were rising to the surface, the comrades were continuing to hammer. Under the flaming rays of the sun, in this morning of youth, it was with this sound that the countryside was heavy. Men were springing up—a black, avenging army was slowly germinating in the furrows, sprouting for the harvests of the coming century. And soon this germination would sunder the earth.[19]

Germinal dates from 1885, and even the historically uninformed can surely sense from passages like this how intimately the novel is bound to sweeping social forces—to the life and death of the Paris Commune, to the looming conflicts between classes, and to all the burgeoning cracks in social fabrics everywhere, produced by ineluctable but only dimly understood forces. Zola's French consciously evokes these immense, grinding changes, and the Hochmans' translation nicely evokes Zola's all-too imitable style. Their paragraph contains twelve sentences, eleven of them declarative, and only the third interrogative. There are distinctly fewer commas, twenty-three instead of thirty-five (reasonably predictable in twentieth-century translations of nineteenth-century novels); more important, with the exception of the final, twelfth sentence, split off from Zola's final sentence, as in the original every sentence is broken by some form of punctuation. (Sentence 2 uses a dash, a punctuation mark of which our century is more fond than was the century just before us; sentence 11 uses a dash plus two commas.) Nor are any of the sentences dramatically longer than others, so that the tumbling and pouring of Zola's style is well reproduced. We will turn to lexicon shortly, to see how predictive this tracking of syntactic movement may be. But first there are two other translations to be considered:

And beneath his feet, the deep blows, those obstinate blows of the pick, continued. The mates were all there; he heard them following him at every stride. Was not that Maheude beneath the

19. Trans. Stanley Hochman and Eleanor Hochman (New York: Signet, 1970), 428.

beetroots, with bent back and hoarse respiration accompanying the rumble of the ventilator? To left, to right, farther on, he seemed to recognize others beneath the wheatfields, the hedges, the young trees. Now the April sun, in the open sky, was shining in his glory, and warming the pregnant earth. From its fertile flanks life was leaping out, buds were bursting into green leaves, and the fields were quivering with the growth of the grass. On every side seeds were swelling, stretching out, cracking the plain, filled by the need of heat and light. An overflow of sap was mixed with whispering voices, the sound of the germs expanding in a great kiss. Again and again, more and more distinctly, as though they were approaching the soil, the mates were hammering. In the fiery rays of the sun on this youthful morning the country seemed full of that sound. Men were springing forth, a black avenging army, germinating slowly in the furrows, growing towards the harvest of the next century, and their germination would soon overturn the earth.[20]

Not by any means the worst translation of *Germinal* I have seen, this is nonetheless not as good a reproduction of the original as the Hochmans'. There are eleven sentences, as in Zola; there are twenty-five commas, as in the Hochman version, plus one semicolon. Ten of the sentences are declarative; one interrogative. But several things make the syntactical tracking inconsistent and, thereby, much less effective. Relative uniformity of movement across each and all of the sentences, perhaps the single most important stylistic feature of the French original, is fractured at a number of points: (1) the semicolon of sentence 2 has virtually the interruptive weight of a period, rather than that of a comma (or a single dash); and (2) once relative uniformity is to some extent recaptured, after the third (interrogative) sentence, it is totally and finally disrupted by the flat and stretched penultimate sentence: "In the fiery rays of the sun on this youthful morning the country seemed full of that sound." This sentence marches to a heavily different drummer than anything in Zola. Overall, the French original gives a sense of neatly notched, closely fitting parts working toward a tightly controlled whole; Ellis's translation seems, instead, almost improvised, not entirely focused. His brief "Introduction" informs us that he did not write but spoke the translation, which was then recorded by another hand.[21] That may well be the source of the problem: spoken English is not, as I said earlier, what can be accurately called prose. Neither its syntax nor its lexicon match well with the

20. Trans. Havelock Ellis (1894; reprint, London: Dent, 1946), 403-4.
21. Ibid., vi.

written form of the language. This unusual translation methodology may also account for the disturbing sense of inexactness that hangs over this translation—the lack of focus I mentioned a moment ago. The voice, like the eye, can move quickly between and among assorted objects and ideas of different sorts; the written word must move differently, and Zola's written words move very differently indeed, staying on a single, die-straight track of which Ellis does not seem quite aware. He has not mangled the syntactic movement of the original, but neither has he satisfactorily tracked it.

> Deep down underfoot the picks were still obstinately hammering away. All his comrades were there, he could hear them following his every step. Beneath this field of beet was it not Maheude, bent double at her task, whose hoarse gasps for breath were coming up to him, mingled with the whirring of the ventilator? To left and to right far away into the distance he thought he could recognize other friends under the corn, the hedges and young trees. The April sun was now well up in the sky, shedding its glorious warming rays on the teeming earth. Life was springing from her fertile womb, buds were bursting into leaf and the fields were quickening with fresh green grass. Everywhere seeds were swelling and lengthening, cracking open the plain in their upward thrust for warmth and light. The sap was rising in abundance with whispering voices, the germs of life were opening with a kiss. On and on, ever more insistently, his comrades were tapping, tapping, as though they too were rising through the ground. On this youthful morning, in the fiery rays of the sun, the whole country was alive with this sound. Men were springing up, a black avenging host was slowly germinating in the furrows, thrusting upwards for the harvest of future ages. And very soon their germination would crack the earth asunder.[22]

I cannot deny this paragraph a rhythm of its own; I must however deny that its rhythm reflects the French original. (The wordiness of this translation is not caused by sheer bulk, since its word count (225) matches that of Zola's original, while the Hochmans use 210 words and Ellis 211. A roughly 9 percent difference does not seem particularly significant.) There are, once more, twelve sentences, eleven of them declarative. But there are only seventeen commas in the entire paragraph; the first and last sentences contain none, and sentences 2, 4, 5, 6, 7, and 8

22. Trans. Leonard Tancock (Harmondsworth: Penguin, 1954), 498-99.

contain only one. Were this poetry, we might speak of the "breath line," and I suspect, even though this is the very farthest thing from poetry, we would not be far off to speak of it here as well. The Penguin translator is not even trying to "breathe" along with his original—and whether that unlikeness is displayed in the handling of lexicon and rhetoric too we will now consider.

Zola's first sentence uses its three commas to emphasize three, possibly four words: *pieds* ("feet"), *profonds* ("deep, profound, great, strong"), *obstinés* ("willful, stubborn, persistent, dogged") and, perhaps, *rivelaines* ("miners' picks"). The Hochmans' differently arranged sentence, with but one comma, nevertheless stresses three of these same four: "heavy," "stubborn," "hammering," and "picks." Ellis, with three commas, emphasizes four, possibly five words, most of them once more the same as those emphasized in the original: "feet," "blows," "obstinate," "blows" ("again"), and, perhaps, "pick." The Penguin version, which uses no commas or other internal punctuation markers, seems to be distributing emphasis very widely indeed. I may be in error (and tomorrow I may "scan" this sentence differently), but I count no fewer than seven emphasized words: "deep," "down," the second syllable of "underfoot," "picks," "obstinately," "hammering," and "away." Remarkably, three of these seven stressed words do not occur in the French: "deep," "down," and "hammering." That is, these three very important words are at best interpretative, at worst intrusive. Ellis has no such interpretative renderings; the Hochmans have one, "hammering," which is how, like the Penguin translator, they have chosen to translate *coups* ("blows, strokes").

We too will drown in minutiae if I continue through the passage at this pace. What we have seen in the first sentence is, all in all, what we see throughout. *L'échine cassée* ("spine fractured/crushed"), for example, is "back breaking" in the Hochmans' version, "bent back" in Ellis, but "bent double at her task" in the Penguin translation—an interpretative rendering that manages to be both unfaithful and bowdlerized at the same time. The *ronflement* ("snoring, roaring, booming, pealing") of the mine's ventilating machine is for the Hochmans a "rumbling," for Ellis "a rumble," but for the Penguin translator a bland "whirring." The word *can* mean nothing more than "whirring"; that is one of the many lexical choices any translator can make. To make it here, however, seems both a betrayal of Zola and terribly consistent with what I have characterized as Penguin's consistent editorial preferences.

Ellis alone takes "le soleil d'avril rayonnait dans sa gloire" ("the April sun was shining in its glory") more or less head-on, though he breaks into it with what is, in French, a preceding phrase, "Maintenant, en plein ciel" ("Now, in the full/round sky"): "the April sun . . . was shining in his glory."

The Hochmans have "the April sun ... high in the sky, blazing gloriously." Tepidly, the Penguin translator partially dissociates "glorious" from the April sun: "The April sun was now well up in the sky, shedding its glorious ... rays." Fields in the original are "tresaillaient de la pousée des herbes" ("shiving/shuddering/thrilling/trembling/wincing from the thrust/shoving of the grass"). The Hochmans translate, "fields were trembling under the push of the grass"; Ellis translates, "the fields were quivering with the growth of the grass"; but the Penguin translator shrinkingly gives us only "the fields were quickening with fresh green grass." I do not mean to be harsh, but this sort of subtle disemboweling of a vibrant original can only be termed a kind of sly bowdlerization: no matter what mistakes other translators may make, only the Penguin translators consistently, and apparently deliberately, temper Homer with Trollope. Fecund seeds may *se gonflaient* and *s'allongeaient* ("swell/puff and stretch out/grow longer"), and other more risqué translators may depict the phallic "swelling ... stretching out" (Ellis and the Hochmans), but the Penguin translator is careful to defuse improprieties with "swelling and lengthening"—the latter almost meaningless here. *Hélas,* none of the translators adequately handles the seeds making a *bruit* ("noise") as they "s'épandait en un grand baiser" ("pour out/spread/flow out in a great/ huge/grand kiss"—though it must also be noted that the Larousse French-English dictionary warns "*baiser quelqu'un* is not in decent use," and Geneviève Edis's handbook of French slang explains that *baiser* = "to fuck"[23]). "The sound of seeds spread in a great kiss" (Hochman and Penguin) rather mutes this; "the sound ... expanding in a great kiss" (Ellis) does a bit better. But when "la campagne était grosse" ("the countryside was fat/great/loud") with this same sound, the Hochmans translate "it was with this sound that the countryside was heavy," Ellis translates lamely, "the country seemed full of that sound," and the Penguin version briskly informs us that "the whole country was alive with this sound." That is, the Hochmans are not squeamish, Ellis is just a bit squeamish, but the Penguin version is downright embarrassed (and embarrassing).

Let me turn, now, to my last example, Marcel Proust's towering, multivolume *À la recherche du temps perdu.* Although it is a translation that has since been revised (by Terence Kilmartin), the original and almost complete rendering of the novel, by C. K. Scott Moncrieff, is not only still in print but has yet to have a competitor. The situation will soon change; the best living translator of French into English, Richard Howard, has for

23. *Larousse Modern French-English Dictionary* (Paris: Librairie Larousse, 1960), 65a; Geneviève Edis, *Merde* (New York: Macmillan, 1984), 59.

some time been at work on a new rendering. I do not know what title will be given to the new version; I do not know how the translation will read. What I would like to do, accordingly, is briefly examine what proper handling of Proust's text might require and what treatment that text has so far received. When in due course Richard Howard's translation appears, we will see whether he and I agree.

> Longtemps, je me suis couché de bonne heure. Parfois, à peine ma bougie éteinte, mes yeux se fermaient si vite que je n'avais pas le temps de me dire: "Je m'endors." Et, une demi-heure après, la pensée qu'il était temps de chercher le sommeil m'éveillait; je voulais poser le volume que je croyais avoir encore dans les mains et souffler ma lumière; je n'avais pas cessé en dormant de faire des réflexions sur ce que je venais de lire, mais ces réflexions avaient pris un tour un peu particulier; il me semblait que j'étais moi-même ce dont parlat l'ouvrage: une église, un quatuor, la rivalité de François Premier et de Charles-Quint.

If Flaubert is a chief stylistic model for the nineteenth century, clearly Proust occupies a similar position for the twentieth. The passage just quoted, which begins the novel, is of course from what, in English, is called *Swann's Way* and, in French, is *Du côté de chez Swann.* As I have noted, Scott Moncrieff, faced with the overall title, *À la recherche du temps perdu* ("In search of lost/ruined/wasted time"), cut what he apparently saw as a Gordian knot and substituted the famous Shakespearian phrase, "remembrance of things past." There are a myriad other possibilities, one or more of which may someday be attached to the Englishing of Proust's novel: "in search of lost time," "in search of buried time," "in search of the past," and so on. Similarly, since *chez Swann* means "at Swann's home," or "at home with Swann," and *à côté de* means "near, beside, next to, by the side of," there are clearly viable alternatives to *Swann's Way.* Whether they will ever be invoked is anyone's guess.

What Proust demonstrates, even in these three sentences, is a deft, practiced, immensely authoritative command of the vast resources of the French language, its structure(s) and lexicon not least of all. He begins with an eight-word sentence, divided, resonantly, into a profoundly governing one-word opening, "Longtemps" ("for long, for a long time"), set off by a comma and followed by a straightforward and brief seven-word main clause, "je me suis couché de bonne heure" ("I went to sleep/bed early/in good time"). Beginning sentence 2 similarly, with "Parfois" ("sometimes, now and then, occasionally, at times"), he lets the structure unfold a bit, ending with a colon and the short utterance, placed in speech-like quotation marks, "Je m'endors" ("I'm falling asleep/I'm dropping off"). It is only sentence 3 (with its three full clauses set off by semicolons, and its final phrase, a typical Proustian list signaled by a colon) which introduces us to the sorts of complex prose structures he intends to use in shaping and elaborating a novel truly unlike any other in the genre's long history. Neither his style nor the book's unique construction are imitable, though they have certainly been and will continue to be deeply influential—and for the translation of such a novel, perhaps above all others, tracking syntactic movement is essential.

On the whole, Scott Moncrieff shapes his English version very much the way Proust has shaped the original:

> For a long time I used to go to bed early. Sometimes, when I had put out my candle, my eyes would close so quickly that I had not even time to say to myself: "I'm falling asleep." And half an hour later the thought that it was time to go to sleep would awaken me; I would make as if to put away the book which I imagined was still in my hands, and to blow out the light; I had gone on thinking, while I was asleep, about what I had just been reading, but these thoughts had taken a rather peculiar turn; it seemed to me that I myself was the immediate subject of my book: a church, a quartet, the rivalry between François I and Charles V.[24]

The number of sentences is the same; the relative lengths, and the differing complexities, of those sentences are in most respects the same; and thus a good deal of Proust's style has been preserved. But not all. For one thing, what seems to me the extremely important initial "Longtemps," followed by perhaps as weighty and significant a comma as any writer has ever employed, is eliminated in the translation. This also eliminates the parallelism between "Longtemps," at the start of sentence 1, and "Parfois," at the start of sentence 2. We can dispute till the end of time the real importance of either or both these losses. I would however argue that, in translating a great book by any great prose stylist, every detail that can be transmitted ought to be transmitted. All details are like interlocking threads, woof and warp of the final fabric and inseparable from it. No detail in such a book is inessential; no detail should be gratuitously omitted. This is a very strong statement, but I do not think I am taking a

24. Trans. C. K. Scott Moncrieff, rev. Terence Kilmartin (New York: Random House, 1981; reprint, New York: Vintage, 1989), 3. I cite this rather than the older, unrevised edition because no changes have been made in the passage cited, and it has thus, in a sense, been co-opted.

stance of illegitimate or unctuous literary piety. A translator can perhaps argue quite reasonably, in most situations, that he is entitled to judge what works and what does not work in the language into which he or she is translating; the original author, after all, did not write in that language and almost invariably could not have. I have myself taken that position, and more than once. But a book as great and important as Proust's, or (as I shall maintain in the last chapter of this book) Cervantes' *Don Quijote,* is not like other books: its power and influence are not only unique, which by definition means inimitable, but they are essential. There is that in such books—there are of course not many of them—which is humanly necessary: in a sense, they have something approaching a kind of scriptural authority. And just as copyists of the Koran were not permitted to make mistakes (mistakes in transmitting so holy a text being both inconceivable and intolerable, copyists who perpetrated errors were summarily executed), and the manuscript tradition was thus kept inviolate, so too, I believe, must be the inter-language transmission of such truly Great Books. (I am to be sure not in favor of capital punishment for linguistic error.)

Scott Moncrieff's handling of lexicon is similarly not quite what one would like. French has a different and far more precise tense structure than English; the "historical past" (*le passé simple*) and the "continuing past" (*le passé imparfait*) express different chronological realities, just as the *subjonctif* (subjunctive mood) still exists and still is used, in French, to "indicate that an action is conceived as subordinate to some other action and, therefore, as something doubtful."[25] "I used to go to bed early" distinctly suggests that the original is in the *passé imparfait*—but it is not. "À peine ma bougie éteinte" ("My candle barely/scarcely extinguished") is not well rendered as "when I had put out my candle." One can excuse the faintly tautological "even" added to the rendering of "je n'avais pas le temps" ("I hadn't the time"); one can understand turning "chercher le sommeil" ("hunt/look for sleep") into "go to sleep," there being in truth no English idiom quite like the French. (Though it might be possible for a devoted translator to devise an equivalent: like Thomas Mann, I believe in both the power and the necessity of translating, even though, as he put it, "It is *fundamentally impossible.*"[26]) Perhaps

25. *Nouveau Petit Larousse Illustré: Dictionnaire Encyclopédique* (Paris: Librairie Larousse, 1933), 989a; my translation. Lest I offend grammarians, who can be a tetchy lot, let me append (and considering for whom I do so, I will not translate) this more complete explanation: "Il y a cinq temps dans le verbe français pour exprimer le passé: l'*imparfait,* le *passé simple,* le *passé composé,* le *passé antérieur* (qui exprime qu'une chose à eu lieu immédiatement avant une autre: *hier, quand j'eus diné, je sortis*), et le *plus-que-parfait.*" Ibid., 752a–752b.

26. Quoted in Burton Raffel, *The Art of Translating Poetry* (University Park: Pennsylvania State University Press, 1988), 11.

one can even excuse translating "poser le volume" ("put down the tome/volume"—there is a perfectly good and familiar French word for book, *le livre,* and Proust knew it as well as anyone) as "put away the book," though I am not happy with such a rendering. But "faire des réflexions" ("mull over/make reflections about") is quite limply translated as "thinking . . . about," and Scott Moncrieff adds to the difficulty by turning the second iteration of *réflexions* into "thoughts." Repetition is both a risky and an important part of stylistics. When I teach writing, I emphasize that every repetition ought either to be "incremental"—that is, to add something—or be omitted. Proust felt this repetition warranted; I do not think his translator ought to deny him the right to make such decisions. Conversely, where a word such as *quatuor* ("string quartet") has a very specific and limited meaning in French (what one calls, in law, a "term of art"), I do not think the translator should turn it into a generalized word like "quartet." A quartet of *what?* The French original, as I have noted, tells you. Scott Moncrieff does not, and he should have.

I do not mean to underestimate the difficulty of Scott Moncrieff's tasks. John Tusa, managing director of the BBC World Service, once addressed aspects of that difficulty in a wise and witty essay, one brief excerpt from which will nicely end this chapter:

> Finnish thought processes—not merely word order—are significantly different from their European neighbors. We are not handling verbal jigsaws: the world looks different in a different tongue. . . . Finnish . . . is a very down-to-earth language, with a maddening shortage of abstract nouns. There is no definite or indefinite article. There is only one personal pronoun doing duty for both "he" and "she." Nouns have fifteen declensions, of which some thirteen are currently used. Some nouns can on occasion be used in a comparative or superlative mode, like adjectives. Verbs have four infinitives, some of which can be declined as nouns! Present tense has to cover also future, continuous, intended or habitual action.[27]

---

27. John Tusa, "And nation shall speak unto nation?" *Times Literary Supplement,* 8 May 1992, 13-14. The essay is a treasure trove of seriously hilarious illustrative material.

PART

2

Translating Rabelais
and Cervantes

5

Translating Rabelais

"I am large," Walt Whitman informed us, "I contain multitudes." But it would surely be easier to translate a multitudinous Whitman into French than to encircle the literally enormous heft of Rabelais and linguistically transport that enormous bulk into English. Nor am I speaking of the sheer physical size of either writer's books: literary weight is not a function of poundage, and spiritual heft does not depend on word count. For just as Whitman's "multitudes" are the many phases of Walt himself, so too the largeness in Rabelais is Rabelais—and it does no discredit to Whitman to recognize that Rabelais's breadth and range are incomparably large. Indeed, the chief sustaining factor for the translator, as it is the principal thread that holds together at least the first four books of *Gargantua and Pantagruel* (the fifth, about which scholars and others have disputed for more than four hundred years, is plainly not fully finished writing; if it is truly Rabelais's work, as I think it probably is, it is without question patched together out of drafts and discarded or unfinished pages), is the vibrant, pounding large-heartedness that makes any and all effort worthwhile, even in the cause of adolescent humor, even in the cause of brain-numbing Jabberwockism, even in the cause of hopelessly outdated and sometimes incomprehensible scholastic wit, even in the cause of stunning female phobias and

Renaissance cruelties and barbarities and an overriding inability to restrain not only a passion for excremental dabbling but, in truth, to restrain anything. Once Rabelais takes a bone in his teeth, you know it will be not only well-chewed, but thoroughly gummed, licked, sniffed, tongued, gnawed, slobbered over, and generally worn to a powder. It does not matter: nothing embarrasses Rabelais, nor should it, for his toweringly human warmth overspreads everything just as powerfully and, yes, with all the same sacred force and effect, as Gerard Manley Hopkins's Holy Ghost, brooding "over the bent / World . . . with warm breast and . . . bright wings."[1] Like his fictional giants, father and son, Rabelais is a giant Humanist, a great Christian, and neither he nor his translator need ever apologize to anyone for anything. Nor are these words of mere puffery, inserted at the start of this chapter for rhetorical effect: Rabelais's translators, unfortunately, have all too often felt it necessary to subdue or change his meaning in the interests of the squeamish standards of another age. One of the anonymous but conclusively academic pre-publication reviewers of my translation, uneasy that Rabelais's characters keep exclaiming—for all the world like men of the late twentieth century—"Bren!"[2] and that I kept translating this exclamation, straightforwardly, "Shit!" asked unhappily if I couldn't, please, at least sometimes change this to what he considered the more innocuous "Crap!" And as we shall see, bowdlerization of François Rabelais's magnificently impolite book has gone, alas, much farther even than that counsel of pained timidity (as well as linguistic incompetence, for what living speaker of the language has ever been heard to exclaim, in the sense of "Damn!" "The Hell you say!" or even "Holy Cow!" a respectable, sanitized "Crap"?).

From the very start—the first phrases of the first sentence of the prologue to what is always now printed as the first book (*Gargantua*) of his gigantic, sprawling novel—Rabelais, sublimely, gloriously indifferent to all standards, conventions, and restrictions, makes nothing easy. "Beuveurs très illustres," he begins, "et vous, véroléz très précieux" ("Exceedingly illustrious drinkers, and you, tremendously precious syphilitics")—and how does one properly translate *véroléz,* which does indeed mean, say all the dictionaries, persons infected with syphilis? There are, it seems to me, two distinctly different approaches:

1. "God's Grandeur," in *The Poems of Gerard Manley Hopkins,* 4th ed., rev. and enlarged, ed. W. H. Gardner and N. H. MacKenzie (London: Oxford University Press, 1970), 66.

2. *Rebut, ordure, excréments* ("garbage/trash, excrement/dung"), *Dictionnaire de l'ancien français jusqu'au milieu du XIVème siècle,* ed. A.-J. Greimas (Paris: Librairie Larousse, 1980), 82b.

1. Translate what the word means
2. Translate what the word meant

What underlies this chronologically oriented distinction, to be sure, is the unspoken but vital premise that the first choice (the present tense, "means") will produce synchronic (contemporary) signification, while the second choice (the past tense, "meant") will evoke diachronic (historical) signification. But the distinction is hardly clear-cut, and I wavered from one approach to the other. Rabelais and his time knew that "the pox," as it was called in then-contemporary English, was a disease of some annoying seriousness and that it seemed to be sexually transmitted. They did not, however, fully understand either its etiology, its nature, or its devastating results; what we now know as third-stage syphilis, for example, and call paresis, was then known only as part of a large and ill-defined malady termed "palsy," which had not yet been connected to syphilis. It was not until 1905 that science established a clear distinction between syphilis and the vexatious but—still today—rather lightly taken "clap," or gonorrhea.[3] No reader of Rabelais can doubt that, for him, both drinking and sexual carousing were unequivocally good things. And he emphatically expresses his affection for and approval of drinkers and pox-sufferers, as this first sentence of the prologue continues, by declaring roundly that "à vous, non à aultres, sont dédiéz mes escriptz" ("to you, not to anyone else, my writings are dedicated"). In Rabelais's mind, as his book bears abundant witness, to be a good drinker was a good thing because affection for wine (in particular) was an important indicator of masculine prowess and worth; to have the pox was also a good thing, because affection for (or at least sexual encounters with) women counted as yet another sign of masculine prowess and worth.

In short, the lexical identification of "the pox" with "syphilis" is to some extent specious, for to Rabelais the former was something of a lark and, as we have since learned, the latter is no joke at all. Long after Rabelais's day, syphilis was best known not only as "the pox" but "the French pox." Significantly, the word "syphilis" does not occur in English until 1686, and does not seem to have taken hold until 1718; "syphilis" did not even exist as a word until 1530, toward the latter part of Rabelais's life, when it appeared in a Latin poem composed by an Italian physician, Jerome Fracastor. Another Italian physician, Giovanni di Vigo, bears testimony to the then prevailing attitude toward the disease, even among doctors (somewhat better informed than the populace at large:

3. *Van Nostrand's Scientific Encyclopedia,* 5th ed., ed. Douglas M. Considine (New York: Van Nostrand, 1976), 2146a: "Development of the darkfield microscope made it possible for the first time to detect the causative spirochete."

Rabelais was of course himself a physician). Describing the symptoms experienced by his patients, di Vigo wrote in 1514 that "after a long time, malignant [i.e., 'bad'] ulcers appeared and are hard to cure."[4] That which is merely "hard to cure" is not to be feared as, today, we fear syphilis.

Accordingly, as is so often the case, the translator who wishes to be totally accurate must consider not only his author, and what his author intended to convey to an audience of his contemporaries but also the audience for which the translation is meant, and what his choice will convey to that audience. At that point the responsible twentieth-century translator of Rabelais realizes that he cannot impose on his sixteenth-century author the burden of the knowledge, and the accompanying set of emotions, present in even medically ill-informed twentieth-century minds. "Pox" rather than "syphilis" as the translation for *vérolez* thus becomes inevitable—though it is perhaps fair to wonder what lexical choice some putative future translator might make if in his or her time the state of medical knowledge had regressed and was once more essentially identical with that of the sixteenth century. In any event, the twentieth-century translator's decision about the proper translation of *vérolez* clearly cannot be dictated only by narrow lexical or even by broader linguistic concerns but must take into account a larger mixture of vectors, necessarily including historical and cultural issues that can be, as here they plainly are, of a certain complexity.

The first page of the prologue, like virtually every page of Rabelais, is sprinkled with problems large and small. We have lost (or misplaced) an enormous body of knowledge that Rabelais tacitly assumed he and his readers shared. Nor is this difficulty simply a matter of the changes effected by time, for as Professor Screech well says, "Rabelais was never a popular author. . . . Uneducated contemporaries . . . could never have understood a tithe of what he wrote in the *Tiers Livre* [Third Book] . . . [and] even *Pantagruel* and *Gargantua* [the early books] assume knowledge available exclusively to the Latin-educated who were sympathetic to Hebrew and Greek culture."[5] In still more specific terms, "Rabelais [often assumed] . . . that his readers all have a sound knowledge of Latin, an aspiring knowledge of Greek, a smattering of Hebrew, a genuine knowledge of Roman law, an acquaintance with Renaissance medical or philosophical commonplaces and, indeed, a grasp of the whole encyclopaedia of Renaissance learning."[6]

4. Quoted in Geoffrey Marks and William K. Beatty, *Epidemics* (New York: Charles Scribner's Sons, 1976), 114.
5. M. A. Screech, *Rabelais* (Ithaca: Cornell University Press, 1979), 12.
6. Ibid., xiii.

But these are, in spite of their importance, reasonably obvious difficulties. They must be surmounted even to read Rabelais, and yet overcoming them does not begin to solve all the translator's problems, many of which are not only hidden from the reader who cannot decipher the original but are frequently undetected even by the scholarly reader who can. Worse still, they are frequently not apparent even to translators. When Rabelais writes, for example, that Socrates, "sans controverse prince des philosophes" ("without any argument the prince of philosophers"), was to say the least an unprepossessing figure, one of the points he makes is that Socrates was "toujours beuvant d'autant à un chascun" ("always drinking, besides, with anyone [and everyone]"). It is harder than it seems, a great deal harder, to get Rabelais's full meaning into English, even with so deceptively simple a phrase. Let me cite chapter and verse. Here are the major renderings of this phrase in three versions, the first being the earliest English translation, followed by the two most recent complete translations before my own:

"carousing to every one"[7]

"forever drinking neck to neck with his friends"[8]

"always drinking glass for glass with everybody"[9]

Of these three renderings, only the seventeenth-century version does not translate *beuvant* (drinking) both literally and flatly; it is thus the only one of these translations which goes beyond the merely lexical meaning at issue and, in the process, by penetrating (in Ezra Pound's terms) to "wot [Rabelais] *means,*" becomes the only one of these three that does justice to the original. The question is, What is Rabelais here describing? Is it the everyday act of calmly imbibing, say, a glass of water—the sort of thing most usually indicated by the English word "drinking"? When in Richard Wagner's *Die Walküre* the exhausted hero, Siegmund, rouses himself from his prone, motionless position and calls out, "Ein Quell! Ein Quell!" using a highly charged poetic expression to ask for something like "a cooling draught from a spring," can we rightly translate what the hero has asked for as a mere "drink"?[10] There are

7. Trans. Thomas Urquhart and Peter Le Motteux, 1653 [for books 1 and 2; book 3 appeared in 1693; books 4 and 5 in 1694], ed. A. J. Nock and C. R. Wilson (New York: Harcourt, Brace, 1931), vol. 1, 199.

8. Trans. Jacques Le Clerq (1936; reprint, New York: Modern Library, 1944), 3.

9. Trans. J. M. Cohen (Harmondsworth: Penguin, 1955), 37.

10. Andrew Porter's British translation of the opera's libretto, alas, does so translate: Richard Wagner, *The Ring of the Nibelung,* trans. Andrew Porter (London: Faber, 1976), 77b.

three or four perfectly good German words (such as *Getränk, Trunk, Schluck*) for "drink," many of them incorporating such added associations as are carried by "potion, draft, gulp," and so on. But none of these words have exactly the soaring, high poetic associations of *quell,* nor will you likely find *quell* listed under "drink," in an English-German *Wörterbuch.* (Even the not overly bright Sieglinde, having quickly fetched water in a drinking horn, understands matters well enough to explain, when she returns, that she has brought "refreshment for the parched roof of the mouth" ("Labung . . . dem lechzenden Gaumen").[11] "Carouse" no longer expresses for us what it conveyed in the sixteenth and seventeenth centuries. The *OED* records that, as a verb, "carouse" then had the sole, specific, and very pointed meaning of "to drink 'all out', drink freely and often," and as a noun carried the plain sense of "a drinking bout."[12] That, indeed, is the sort of "drinking" Rabelais intends to invoke for his readers. "Drinking neck to neck with his friends," Le Clerq's rather garrulous invention, works hard—harder than it should—to convey Rabelais's true meaning, but cannot overcome the damping effect of his crucially bland word choice, "drinking," no matter how many other words he piles on top of it. Even the Penguin translator, J. M. Cohen, though he demonstrably has no feeling for style (as we shall see, not just Rabelais's style but *style,* per se) flails about to try to heighten his defective word choice. But "drinking glass to glass with everybody" not only has the failings of a bland verb, it unfortunately lacks the easy movement of idiomatic English. And since whatever other deficiencies may have been laid to his door, Rabelais never lacks linguistic ease, to make him thump and clump where he should flow and soar is bad translation, plain and simple. My own rendering, finally, is "always chugging down glass after glass with anyone who came along." This is, in late twentieth-century (American) English, precisely what I understand Rabelais to have said, in his own mid-sixteenth-century version of French. Note that, just as "chugging down" evokes the required clinking-and-clanking ambiance of Rabelais's *beuvant,* much as "carousing" did for seventeenth-century (British) English, so too "glass *after* glass" (emphasis added) both conveys the briskly continuing nature of the process and also avoids the stiff, unidiomatic movement of "glass to glass"—a phrase that, in the intended sense, fits comfortably in no one's mouth. By definition, again, no phrase that does not fit comfortably in the mouth belongs in Rabelais. Not that he is writing

11. Which Porter doggedly turns into "Cool your lips with this drink that I've brought you!" Wagner is not the greatest poet in the world, but surely he does not deserve such gross mistreatment.

12. For convenience of citation, see the condensed, one-volume edition, *The Oxford Universal Dictionary . . . ,* 3rd. ed., rev. (Oxford: Oxford University Press, 1955), 267c.

"oral" French: as I have said, his is frequently a learned style, without any doubt written for others as learned as himself. Rather, to quote Professor Screech once more, "Not for centuries, if ever, had anyone in Rabelais's class as a scholar and thinker devoted his comic talents to making learned laughter so open and so vastly enjoyable."[13] And "always drinking glass for glass with everybody" is prose that is by no one's standards "vastly enjoyable." As I said more than twenty years ago in my first book on this subject, and have been insisting ever since, "If [the translator] chooses to translate in the first place, he is required to choose well in translating."[14]

Rabelais's mind-shape, as displayed in the syntactic movement in this, the very first of his paragraphs the reader sees (again, not the first written: *Pantagruel* appeared in 1532 and, being an enormous success, promptly resulted in *Gargantua,* published—no one is entirely sure—in either 1534 or 1535), is fully typical. That is, the kind of headlong forward movement, embellished with turns this way and that, is not only precisely what one would expect of history's first "Rabelaisian," it is in fact precisely what one gets:

> Silènes estoient jadis petites boites, telle que voyons de présent ès bouticques des apothecaires, pinctes au-dessus de figures joyeuses et frivoles, comme de harpies, satyres, oysons bridéz, lièvres cornuz, canes bastées, boucqs volans, cerfz limonniers et aultres telles pinctures contrefaictes à plaisir pour exciter le monde à rire (quel fut Silène, maistre du bon Bacchus); mais au dedans l'on réservoit les fines drogues comme baulme, ambre gris, amomon, musc, zivette, pierreries et aultres choses précieuses.

The tumbling multiplicity of sensual flashpoints, the open, joyous caressing of words and things and the world, is the hallmark of Rabelais's writing throughout. It is hard not to believe that such exultant prose is a fairly close replication of the man himself. One of the worst things a translator can do to such a tumultuous style is to ignore its syntactic movement and reduce it to a kind of hopping and skipping:

> Sileni, in the days of yore, were small boxes such as you may see nowadays at your apothecary's. They were named for Silenus, foster father to Bacchus. The outside of these boxes bore gay, fantastically painted figures of harpies, satyrs, bridled geese, hares with gigantic horns, saddled ducks, winged goats in flight, harts

13. Screech, 102.

14. Burton Raffel, *The Forked Tongue: A Study of the Translation Process* (The Hague: Mouton, 1971), 23.

in harness and many other droll fancies. They were pleasurably devised to inspire just the sort of laughter Silenus, Bacchus' master, inspired.

But inside these sileni, people kept priceless drugs such as balsam of Mecca, ambergris from the sperm whale, amomum from the cardamom, musk from the deer and civet from the civet's arsehole—not to mention various sorts of precious stones, used for medical purposes, and other invaluable possessions.[15]

Le Clerq's *words* have genuine energy, though there are far too many of them and an almost alarming percentage come, not from Rabelais's French, but from the translator's reference books and his obsessive need to explain everything. Rabelais says, for example, *jadis* ("once, long ago"), and it is rendered "in the days of yore." Rabelais says "lièvres cornuz" ("hares with horns"); it is translated "hares with *gigantic* horns" (emphasis added). Rabelais says *ambre gris* (ambergris), and Le Clerq gives us both a translation and a schoolbook lesson: "ambergris from the sperm whale." This is, literally (and sometimes at quite enormous length), an encyclopedic translation. But the *mind* we meet, in this sort of translation (which chops one Rabelaisian sentence into five, and cuts part of a long paragraph into two separate small ones), has a translucent clarity, a simple, orderly movement from point to point, which is about as false a representation as can be. There is surely method in Rabelais's madness, and a high order of intelligence, but inebriation neither is nor wants to be a model of clarity.

Now a Silenus, in ancient days, was a little box, of the kind we see to-day in apothecaries' shops, painted on the outside with such gay, comical figures as harpies, satyrs, bridled geese, horned hares, saddled ducks, flying goats, stags in harness, and other devices of that sort, light-heartedly invented for the purpose of mirth, as was Silenus himself, the master of good old Bacchus. But inside these boxes were kept rare drugs, such as balm, ambergris, cardamum, musk, civet, mineral essences, and other precious things.[16]

There is a reasonably close representation of the externals, here—two sentences, one of them fairly long, instead of one quite long sentence broken by a semicolon—but virtually nothing of Rabelais's energy and vitality has survived. There are, I think, two reasons, one essentially

15. Trans. Le Clerq, 3.
16. Trans. Cohen, 37.

lexical, the other more profound. Lexically, Cohen seems determined to deflate, to flatten, whenever and wherever he conveniently can. (This is I suspect not a conscious and certainly not a malicious intent, but simply a constitutional one; earlier in his career, significantly, Cohen not only translated books for but helped the founding editor, E. V. Rieu, edit and shape the nature of the Penguin Classics series.) "Aultres telles pinctures" ("other such paintings"), writes Rabelais, and Cohen translates "other devices of that sort." "Devices" are not "paintings," especially in modern English; any attempt to construe the word as a term of art used by painters is smothered by the overriding contemporary signification, "something constructed or devised." Cohen seems unaware that to bring forward a secondary meaning the reader must be signaled, prepared, made aware. "Of that sort," more seriously, is terribly offhand translation, almost indeed condescending and certainly indifferent. Rabelais is of course none of those things, neither here nor elsewhere. Cohen's translation, unfortunately, again and again reflects such attitudes, including the horrendous rendering, here, of "contrefaictes à plaisir pour exciter le monde à rire (quel fut Silène, maistre du bon Bacchus)" ("invented for fun/pleasure in order to move/rouse the world to laughter [according to the nature of Silenus, good/honest Bacchus's master]"). "Light-heartedly invented," reads this rendition, "for the purpose of mirth, *as was Silenus himself,* the master of good old Bacchus" (emphasis added). Did Cohen mean us to read this, as it plainly does read, as an assertion that Silenus is nothing but an invention? If it is not condescension, then it is outright incompetence, for the French does not even hint at anything of the sort. "For the purpose of mirth," for *à plaisir* ("for fun/pleasure"), is once more plodding, dull phrasing that does not come anywhere near the stylistic level of the original. "Good old Bacchus" is so extravagantly nineteenth-century British, in the manner of Charles Dickens (vide *A Christmas Carol,* at the end of which we are assured that Scrooge "became as good a friend, as good a master, and as good a man, as the good old city knew, or any other good old city, town, or borough, in the good old world"[17]), that it quite destroys the pleasant and approving but hardly avuncular "bon Bacchus" ("good/honest Bacchus"). Where Rabelais employs the active voice, which is in both languages stronger, more forceful, Cohen flattens with the passive, which is in both languages weaker, less assertive: "au dedans l'on réservoit" ("they kept") becomes "inside these boxes were kept." *Baulme* can mean either "balm," in general, or "balsam," in particular. It seems plain that Rabelais,

17. Charles Dickens, *A Christmas Carol,* in *Christmas Books by Charles Dickens* (Oxford: Oxford University Press, 1954), 76.

relentlessly concrete, has his heart set on the particular. Cohen, with equally relentless determination, translates, dully, "balm." This is not "wrong," in the basic sense of "erroneous." But it plainly is wrong stylistically, even wrong as an opportunity missed. Rabelais is famous for seizing opportunities, not muffing them.

And so to my own translation:

> A Silenus: those used to be little boxes, the kind you see, today, in drug stores, painted all around with light and happy figures, like harpies, satyrs, bridled geese, hares with horns, saddled ducks, flying goats, stags in harness, and all sorts of such images, invented in good fun, just to make the world laugh (exactly as Silenus used to do, honest Bacchus' master). But what they used to keep inside these boxes were rare medicines like balsam and ambergris, cardamom and melegueta pepper, musk, civet, gemstones, and all kinds of precious stuff.[18]

The rendering of so small a matter as "pinctes au-dessus" ("painted over") shows the sternly leveling disposition of Cohen, in this as in so much else a prototypical Penguin translator. Le Clerq gently energizes what is, after all, basically a straightforward bit of description (to the extent, of course, that anything in Rabelais is truly straightforward): "The outside of these boxes bore..." I have translated "painted all around." But Cohen translates, with his infallible instinct for dull and flat phrasing, "painted on the outside." It is "accurate": that is hardly the issue. (Is it "accurate" to call a "scarlet woman" a "red woman"?) It simply does not reproduce more than the bare shell of the original. Again, though anyone with an ear for English knows the danger of "la plume de ma tante" constructions, doggedly dragging French word order into English, Cohen mechanically renders "maistre du bon Bacchus" "master of... Bacchus." Le Clerq, aware of the necessity to sparkle (though not always entirely sure how to accomplish it), translates "Bacchus' master," which is properly idiomatic; my own version uses the same word order.

A whole is composed of the sum of its parts. No work of human hands is perfect; even the greatest of writers, Rabelais among them, exhibit flaws, and the small-minded delight in dwelling on them. But it is not small-minded to point out a long list of flaws, and emphasize that this is still only the novel's first paragraph. With hundreds

18. François Rabelais, *Gargantua and Pantagruel,* trans. Burton Raffel (New York: Norton, 1990).

and hundreds of pages still to go, a translator who has already sunk this deep in the mire is not likely ever to emerge. Nor is the spirit of the original author.

Before we leave this first paragraph, at long last, let me explain that although *amomon* is clearly the French term, dating back to the thirteenth century, for the spice generally known as "cardamom," with the authority of *Le Petit Robert* I have slightly (and I trust to its gain) expanded my translation of *amomon* to also include another exotic spice, melegueta pepper. "Cardamome," says *Le Petit Robert,* is a "plante d'Asie, dont les graines ont un goût poivré"[19] ("an Asian plant whose seeds taste like pepper"). Some hours of checking back and forth between dictionaries and scientific works persuaded me that in origin, use, and nature these two spices, both well-known to and regularly employed by Frenchmen of Rabelais's day, were indeed sufficiently alike to justify both *Le Petit Robert*'s claim and my subsequent translation, based thereon. I hope there are no chefs outraged by the linkage.

The twentieth-century reader who is intrigued by the prologue, but then half stupefied by the immense poem that dominates and virtually crushes chapter 2 of *Gargantua,* will be introduced in chapter 3 to the Middle Ages run mad—almost a fair characterization of Rabelais. (The 112-line poem seems longer even than it is, *tout court,* because as one editor says of it, "Ce que Rabelais veut dire ici, personne ne l'a compris" ("No one has ever understood what Rabelais means/intends here").[20] The sheer energy of Rabelais's prose is infectious:

> Moiennans lesquelles loys, les femmes vefves peuvent franchement jouer du serrecropière à tous enviz et toutes restes, deux moys après le trespas de leurs mariz.

> And thanks to laws like these, widows can play squeeze-your-ass to their hearts' content (and not just their hearts), and bet the whole bank, for two whole months after their husbands have kicked the bucket.[21]

Whether or not Rabelais coined the term *serrecropière* ("bolting rear-ends together"), as he may well have, is less important, here, than what the

19. *Le Petit Robert: Dictionnaire alphabétique et analogique* (Paris: Société du Nouveau Littré, 1967), 229a.
20. *Rabelais, Oeuvres complètes,* ed. Jacques Boulenger (Paris: Gallimard, 1955), 9 n.1.
21. Trans. Raffel, 15.

translator makes of it.[22] Le Clerq, always eager but not, alas, always seated straight in his saddle, translates "our virtuous widows may... freely indulge in games of grip-crupper."[23] This is neither totally obscure nor, frankly, as good as Urquhart and Le Motteux's dated but straight-forward rendering, "honest widows may... play at the close-buttock game."[24] The problem with the Penguin rendering, unfortunately, is that it reproduces the seventeenth-century translation almost word-for-word: "widows... may play at the close-buttock game."[25] There is nothing wrong, to be sure, in borrowing from prior translators: the wheel does not require continual reinvention. But when we borrow, as when we translate, we must be able to see what is usefully borrowed and what, placed on a twentieth-century page, will reek unpleasantly of the lamp.

"À tous enviz et toutes restes" takes us into even slipperier territory, for these are terms borrowed, lustily enough, directly from a different sort of gaming table. *Enviz* means a "bet," a "challenge" (as well, says Professor Screech, as being "obviously, a pun," since *vit* means "penis"[26]), and "è toutes restes," a banco term, means "to risk everything, to bet the bank." Typically, the translator of Rabelais has to combine, as best he or she is able, the original's mockery of canon law, its invocation of the gaming table, its sexual innuendoes, all in one hopefully suitably rollick-ing phrase. My attempt, again, runs: "to their hearts' content (and not just their hearts), and bet the whole bank." Le Clerq syntactically separates out the two-month legal limit, placing it earlier in his sentence, and ends with a gallant explosion: "with a pig in the poke, heels over head and to their hearts' content."[27] If this is not precisely what Rabelais says, it is surely what he meant. Urquhart and Le Motteux, lively and almost inevi-tably dated—for Rabelais's sixteenth-century French is automatically updated in each new translation, but who bothers to update a translator? —translate "with might and main, and as hard as they can." This is, however, a version which, whatever its merits, curiously neglects both the gaming table and the possible sexual innuendoes. Cohen's Penguin

22. Sainéan quotes Estienne Pasquier (1529–1615) as having said that, between them, Calvin and Rabelais were the two "pères de nostre idiome" ("fathers of our language"). Lazare Sainéan, *La Langue de Rabelais* (1922–23; reprint, Geneva: Slatkine Reprints, 1976), vol. 1, x. Sainéan notes *serrecropière,* briefly, at vol. 2, 310, under the general heading of "Erotica Verba" ("erotic words").

23. Trans. Le Clerq, 14.

24. Trans. Urquhart and Le Motteux, vol. 1, p. 207.

25. Trans. Cohen, p. 47.

26. M. A. Screech, note 52, in François Rabelais, *Gargantua* (Geneva: Librairie Droz, 1970), 35.

27. Le Clerq, 14.

squashes as much life as possible out of the words: "with all their might and at every free moment."[28]

But it is when Rabelais really cuts loose, in a long and then a very short paragraph that end chapter 3, that the reader can see both what our author and his translators are made of. Let me quote, seriatim and without interruption, the original French, my own translation, and the Penguin version:

> Je vous prie par grâce, vous aultres mes bons averlans, si d'icelles en trouvez que vaillent le desbraguetter, montez dessus et me les emenez. Car, si au troisième moys elles engroissent, leur fruict sera héritier du defunct; et, la groisse congnueue, poussent hardiment oultre, et vogue la gualée puis que la panse est pleine!—come Julie, fille de l'empereur Octavian, ne se abandonnoit à ses taboureurs sinon quand elle se sentoit grosse, à la forme que la navire ne reçoit son pilot que premièrement ne soit callafatée et chargée. Et, si personne les blasme de soy faire rataconniculer ainsi suz leur grosse, veu que les bestes suz leur ventrées n'endurent jamais le masle masculant, elles responderont que ce sont bestes, mais elles sont femmes, bein endendentes les beaulx et joyeux menuz droictz de superfection comme jadis respondit Populie, selon le raport de Macrobe *li.ij Saturnal.*
>
> Si le diavol ne beult qu'elles engroissent, il fauldra tortre le douzil, et bouche clouse.

> So I beg you by all that's holy, you upstanding young fellows, if you find any juicy widows worth opening your fly front for, hop up—and ride them over here. Because if they get pregnant by the third month, whatever pops out will inherit from the dead man—and once she's visibly pregnant, they can bang on as hard as they like and what the hell! the stomach's already stuffed full—the way Julia, Emperor Octavian's daughter, would never abandon herself to those who played drumroll on her belly until she knew she was pregnant, just like a cargo ship that won't take on a pilot until she's all freshly caulked up and loaded. And if anyone criticizes them for letting the game go on when they're pregnant, since even animals won't stand for males being male-ish, not while they're carrying their young, well, they'll answer that those are animals, but they're human beings, women who understand perfectly well the beautiful, joyous (if minor) privi-

28. Trans. Cohen, 47.

lege of double impregnation, as Populia put it, once upon a time, according to what Macrobius tells us in book two of his *Saturnalia.*

Anyway, if the devil didn't want them to get pregnant, he'd have to turn off the faucet and shut the hole.[29]

So I beg of you, all my fine lechers, if you find any of these same widows worth the trouble of untying your codpiece, mount them and bring them to me. For if they conceive in the third month, their issue will be the dead man's legal heir; and once the pregnancy is public they may push boldly on, full sail ahead, since the hold is full, after the example of Julia, daughter of the Emperor Octavian, who never gave herself up to her belly-drummers unless she knew that she was pregnant, after the manner of a ship, which does not take on her pilot until she is caulked and loaded. And if anyone reproaches them for allowing themselves to be thus sported with in their pregnancy, seeing that animals never allow the covering male near them when they are big, they will answer that beasts are beasts, but that they are women and fully understand the grand and jolly little rights of superfetation; as Populia answered of old, according to Macrobius' account, in the second book of his *Saturnalia.*

If the deuce doesn't want their bellies to swell, he must twist the spigot and close the hole.[30]

"Je vous prie," begins Rabelais, "par grâce" ("I beg you, by all that's holy/in the name of God"), and Cohen omits "Par grâce," though the juxtaposition of holy and unholy is part and parcel of Rabelais's whole approach. It seems but is not a trivial omission. But there is worse to come. "Lechers" is (a) rhetorically too high-toned and (b) lexically too inaccurate to serve as an adequate rendering of *averlans,* which has more the meaning of "fellows, boys, good-for-nothings [spoken jocularly]." We can debate to the end of time whether *desbraguetter* ("untie/open fly front/codpiece [of breeches]") is better kept archaic, or not, in a late-twentieth-century translation. There are valid things to be said on both sides. But *amener* ("lead/conduct/bring"), closely related to *mener* ("lead/conduct/ride/drive/steer") is far too flabbily rendered here as a monosyllabic "bring." Le Clerq, whose over-strenuous (and not quite English rendering) has the ladies in question "surmounted," which is surely a strange rendering of *montez* ("mounted"), then directs "my friends and

29. Trans. Raffel, 15.
30. Trans. Cohen, 47.

lusty lads all" to "bring them home to me."[31] (Urquhart and Le Motteux translate, with unusual limpness, "get up and bring them to me."[32]) Rabelais speaks of the ladies "au troisième moys . . . engroissent" ("becoming pregnant/great with child in/by the third month"); Cohen neutralizes nature by translating "if they *conceive* in the third month" (emphasis added). *Pousser* ("to push, shove, thrust") can of course be translated as a bland "push," which is of course Cohen's choice. I'm afraid Rabelais has a very specific sort of "pushing" in mind, here, and the translator is obliged to convey Rabelais's rather than the first-listed dictionary meaning. "Suz leur ventrées" ("ride on their bellies") is what pregnant female animals won't let *le masle* ("the male") do, when said males are interested in *masculant* ("being masculine"). Cohen has Rabelais say merely that the females "never allow the covering male near them," surely a doubly neutered phrasing, since proximity is not the issue and "covering" ("in itself something of an obsolete word") tends to obscure rather than plainly express what, with "le masle masculant," Rabelais expresses very clearly indeed. To translate *superfection* ("double impregnation") as "superfetation" is, to my mind, to have run and hid oneself behind the safety of a large, obscure, and totally technical term. Note, too, that although the process in question is "beaulx et joyeuz" ("beautiful and joyous") to Rabelais, for Cohen it is only "grand and jolly."

And to translate *le diavol* (the devil) as "the deuce" may have the arguable sanction of British colloquial usage, in which indeed "the deuce" can mean "the devil." But Rabelais does *not* use a colloquial form of the word; the standard form is *diable* and, as Sainéan indicates, Rabelais here uses, instead, an Italian form, just as throughout the novel he uses a whole battery of other forms of the same word, including quite specifically colloquial usages derived from the Breton (*diole*) and local Parisian slang (*diesble*).[33] But there is unquestionably nothing colloquial about *diavol,* and a translator who, elsewhere, consistently flattens and bowdlerizes can only be understood to be here doing the same thing. Further, although *tortre* (modern French *tordre*) certainly means "to twist," and *douzil* is literally "spigot, faucet," Rabelais clearly here intends, as Screech notes, a *sens libre.* Indeed, Screech's note, in the Droz text, illustrates the precise "free meaning" intended by saying "on tordait le *douzil* en l'enfonçant dans le trou d'une barrique" ("one screws down the spigot when one sticks it into the bung-hole of a large barrel").[34] The particular "spigot" to which Rabelais refers, of course, indeed gets "stuck into" the appropri-

31. Trans. Le Clerq, 14.
32. Trans. Urquhart and Le Motteux, 207.
33. Sainéan, vol. 2, 353–54.
34. "Index Verborum," *Gargantua,* 382.

ate "hole." It does not get "twisted." One can translate a metaphor meta-phorically, as in my own translation I have done. But one must be careful not to destroy, or obfuscate, the basic meaning. To "twist the spigot" pretty clearly tries to obliterate the basic sexual meaning. It is squeamish translation, and the squeamish ought not to be translating Rabelais.

It is certainly true, of course, that Rabelais's prose has many levels, sometimes one piled on top of another. He is no more an orderly stylist than he is an orderly constructor of plots or delineator of character. (Or even of physical size: it has many times been observed that Rabelais's giants are giants when Rabelais remembers they are giants, and essentially normal-sized men when he either forgets they are giants or has no use for their sometime outsized stature.) Rabelais can be straightforwardly for-mal and elegant, in the best high Renaissance style, and his translator must do the best that he or she can to reproduce that classically derived, stately, Humanist prose:

> Père très débonnaire, comme à tous accidens en ceste vie transitoire non doubtéz ne soubsonnéz, nos sens et facultéz ani-males pâtissent plus énormes et empotentes perturbations (voyre jusques à en estre souvent l'âme désemparée du corps, quoyque telles subites nouvelles feussent à contentement et soubhayt), que si eussent auparavant esté propenséz et préveux, ainsi me a grandement esmeu et perturbé l'inopinée venu de vostre escuyer Malicorne. Car je n'espéroys aulcun veior de vos domesticques, ne de vous nouvelles ouyr avant la fin de cestuy nostre voyage. Et facilement acquiesçoys en la doulce recordation de vostre auguste majesté, escripte, voyre certes insculpée et engravée on posterieur ventricule de mon cerveau, souvent au vif me la représentant en sa propre et naïfve figure. (*Le Quart Livre,* chap. 4)

This is the introductory paragraph of a dutiful letter written by Pantagruel to Gargantua, his king and father. The younger man, clearly keenly aware of his responsibilities both as son and subject, and well trained in the best, highly mannered style of an educated Renaissance man, has recently sailed off on a long voyage, taking his princely retinue with him. Gargantua sends a fast messenger vessel after him, whereupon Pantagruel first releases a specially bred pigeon, banded white, which will fly swiftly home and reassure his father that all is well. Then he pens the letter of which I have just quoted the first paragraph.

The long, periodical-clause-ridden first sentence is followed by a grace-fully short second and then, to close the introductory paragraph, a well-turned, intellectually complex but not overlong third and final sentence. The first sentence has five commas (one of them in the middle of a philosophical parenthesis); the second sentence has one comma; the final sentence has three.

Le Quart Livre ("The Fourth Book") is, in general, Rabelais at his absolute best; the writing throughout is supple and resonant; the mood is generally mellow and magisterial. Although some later parts of this letter can be seen as stately parodies, more or less, of the prototypical Renaissance scientifically minded explorer—Pantagruel reporting, for example, on the unicorns and the Scythian reindeer he is sending home for his father's delectation—the bulk of the epistle consists of trope-like, familiar variations on carefully conventional themes, saying once more what everyone already knew but everyone needed to have said again, and again, and again. The translator must work hard to successfully capture the movement of this prose, and its sage, unchallenging tone:

> Most gracious father:
> The unexpected, unforseen events that occur in this transitory life come as a more violent shock to our senses and faculties than do the expected and foreseen. Indeed, sudden surprise may cause death; often the soul forsakes the body, even when the news received satisfies our curiosity and longing.
> The arrival of your esquire Malicorne moved me profoundly, for I had not hoped to see any servant of yours or to hear from you before the conclusion of our journeying. I had had to content myself with the cherished remembrance of your august majesty, a remembrance so deeply engraved upon the hindmost ventricle of my brain that I could conjure up your figure in its true, natural, living form.[35]

Le Clerq's translation brings home yet again how inextricably bound together are substance and form. One paragraph has become three; three sentences have become four, with the addition of an almost-sentence-framing semicolon and a formalized colon in the salutation; the parenthetical interjection has vanished; and a total of nine commas has been replaced by a total of six. The syntactic movement of this translation, accordingly, is relatively short and authoritative: one resonant pronouncement is fairly speedily concluded, and then followed at once by another. This is not the work of a pompous mind; Pantagruel is certainly not shown condescending to his royal father. But neither is he shown in the consciously secondary, dutiful rather than assertive, posture that Rabelais

35. Trans. Le Clerq, 516–17.

has worked so hard to convey. This is equal speaking to equal; Pantagruel does not precisely swagger here, but neither does he, as he does in the original, carefully subordinate himself.

And, to shift to lexical issues, the somewhat inflated rhetorical tone is achieved at pretty much the same cost. Pantagruel's easy, natural (shall we say Shakespearian?) demeanor has been replaced by an insistently elevated (shall we say [Alexander] Pope-like?) formality. Rabelais writes, "comme à tous accidens en ceste vie transitoire" ("as in all the unexpected events/accidents of this transitory life"), and Le Clerq subtly raises the rhetorical stakes: "The unexpected, unforeseen events that *occur* in this transitory life" (emphasis added). The highly formal verb, plus the faintly heavy juxtaposition of "unexpected" and "unforeseen" (piled on top of each other, as it were, because only a comma intervenes), delicately elevate the tone. "Telles subites nouvelles feussent à contentement et soubhayt" ("such unexpected/sudden news may be joyful/satisfying and wished-for") becomes "when the news *received* satisfies our *curiosity and longing*" (emphasis added); the italicized words again overelevate the tone. Arrival of the messenger, in the original, "me a grandement esmeu et perturbé" ("profoundly moved and troubled me"), but Le Clerq's statuesque portrayal leaves no room for Pantagruel to be "troubled," and the translation quietly omits it: "moved me profoundly." Le Clerq is also so unsteady in his grasp of English idiom and tone that he translates "postérieur ventricle" neither technically nor colloquially, but, instead, as the jarringly inappropriate "hindmost ventricle." There is I think much the same unsteady grasp in his rendering of *escuyer* ("squire, esquire, horse-messenger") as the etymologically accurate "esquire" rather than the more comprehensible "page." But perhaps the clearest demonstration of lexical bias is Le Clerq's turning Pantagruel's "la doulce recordation" ("the sweet memory") of his father into "the cherished remembrance."

> My very gracious father, just as our senses and animal faculties suffer larger and more violent perturbations from all the unexpected and unlooked-for accidents which come to us in this transitory life, than from events which we expect and understand are coming (indeed, how often the soul takes leave of the body, even though such unexpected news may be joyful and exactly what is wished for), so the unexpected arrival of your page, Malicorne, has deeply moved and even troubled me. For I had no expectation of seeing any of your servants, or of hearing any news of you, before the end of this voyage of mine. And I was readily accustoming myself to the sweet memory of your august majesty, written—no, truly sculpted and engraved deep in the

back portion of my brain, so that it has often re-created for me the very living, authentic image of you.[36]

One of the most delicate rhetorical touches in the original French is how Pantagruel introduces the notion of the father's image being forever implanted in the son's brain: "escripte, voyre certes insculpée et engravée" ("written—in fact/truly most certainly sculpted and engraved"). The syntactic force of "voyre certes" is such that I have used an interrupting dash to register its effect: "written—no, truly sculpted and engraved." But Le Clerq says only "so deeply engraved." The Pantagruel he projects for us is too certain of himself to indulge in the original's rhetorical heaping up of praise. I think it clear that his Pantagruel is not, alas, Rabelais's.

The Pantagruel we find in the Penguin translation is however still less like the original, for he is truly a pompous bore:

> Most gracious Father,
>   The unexpected arrival of your squire Malicorne has greatly moved and affected me. For our senses and faculties suffer more violent and overwhelming surprises in this transitory life from unsuspected and unforseen events than from those expected and anticipated. In fact, the soul is often reft from the body by such shocks, even though the sudden news may be as satisfactory as we could wish. I did not expect to see any of your servants, or to hear any news from you before the end of this voyage of ours. Indeed, I was quietly contenting myself with the sweet memory of your august Majesty, which is so deeply inscribed—or rather sculpted and engraved—on the hindmost lobe of my brain, that often I have been able to call up your likeness in its true living shape.[37]

Cohen uses only two paragraphs, to Le Clerq's three (and Rabelais's one), but he quite destroys the syntactic movement by substituting four short and rather choppy sentences for the flowing periodic clauses of the original's first two sentences. Significantly, his syntactic tracking of the third sentence (the fifth, in his translation) improves, and along with it both the handling of lexicon and the replication of something more like the original's true movement and tone. But this comes too late: the monstrous mouthful constructed in Cohen's second sentence has utterly destroyed both the accuracy of his portrayal and also all reader interest in what Pantagruel may have to say: "For our senses and faculties

36. Trans. Raffel, 399-400.
37. Trans. Cohen, 458.

suffer more violent and overwhelming surprises in this transitory life
from unsuspected and unforeseen events than from those expected and
anticipated." Note how entirely consistent it is for Cohen to translate
"nos sens et facultéz animales" ("our senses and animal faculties") by
suppressing that which is "animal," and to turn *désemparée* ("quit,
abandon") into the futilely archaic "reft."[38] Note too that although Rabelais
has Pantagruel's adjustment to separation from his father come to him
facilement ("readily/easily"), Cohen transmutes this straightforward accep-
tance into a kind of quietist resignation: his Pantagruel makes the adjustment "quietly." I do not think Pantagruel's creator would recognize him.

There are no easy pages in Rabelais, but perhaps the hardest of all, at
least for the translator, are those long sequences in which time has
eroded much of the sense (and in particular the wit and humor), or
when, worse still, Rabelais never intended there to be any sense and what
the translator must confront is deliberate and almost total lack of meaning.
The epitome of humor that dates itself most quickly is of course topical
humor—references to contemporary events, contemporary personages,
and contemporary attitudes, all of which have long ceased to be either
contemporary or even comprehensible. It's much like the little boy who
heard an adult associate Paul McCartney with the Beatles and asked,
surprised, "Oh? Was Paul McCartney in a band before Wings?" Except
that, almost half a millennium later, far more that was common, readily
available knowledge has inevitably passed into the dust-bin (garbage
pail) of history. There are innumerable points in *Gargantua and Pantagruel*
at which, without some help, the late-twentieth-century reader will be
lost. Comments interpolated into a text, in brackets (to excuse the
original author of any responsibility for them), tend to burden the text;
footnotes burden it still more.[39] For the most part, rather than take the
encyclopedic approach employed by Le Clerq, I have preferred either to
add to the text proper a word or two that at least key the uninformed
reader how he can go about informing himself, or to quietly change a
word or two, in the interests of clarity. If for example Rabelais refers to
Saint Paul, as he does, as "le saincte Envoyé" ("the Holy Messenger/the
Blessed Apostle"), I have translated "Blessed Saint Paul."[40] Nothing (or
very little which could be transmitted) is lost, and much (clarity) is
gained. The reader should not be penalized for not having been born in
the sixteenth century and educated in a monastery. (Cohen translates

38. The *OED.*, no Johnny-come-lately among dictionaries, says flatly "Now only *arch.* or
poet." See, again, *The Oxford Universal Dictionary*, 1668a. Pantagruel's letter may have
been penned in the sixteenth century, but it is neither *arch.* nor *poet.*

39. But see Chapter 5, below.

40. *Le Tiers Livre,* chap. 35, trans. Raffel, 334.

"The Holy Apostle," as do Urquhart and Le Motteux, though the modern edition of the latter feels obliged to add an explanatory footnote; Le Clerq translates "the holy apostle Paul."[41]) If Rabelais attributes a saying to Heraclitus (*Tiers Livre,* chap. 36), and should have attributed it, instead, to Democritus, I have simply translated what Rabelais wrote, for who knows whether the "mistake" was conscious or not? This particular mistake occurs twice in the novel, made the first time by Pantagruel (*Pantagruel,* chap. 13), the second by Panurge, and the author's attitudes toward these two characters are very different: Rabelais often mocks Panurge, but not Pantagruel, the major figure in four of the novel's five books. When however Rabelais in the *Tiers Livre,* chap. 27, refers to "le roydde dieu des jardins" (mod. French *raide,* "the stiff king of gardens"), and "stiff" really means "stiff-limbed," and "limbs" includes what some translators refer to, if absolutely forced to mention it, as "the virile member," meaning "penis," and the reference, furthermore, is to the god Priapus (though Rabelais does not think he needs to say so, for the benefit of the audience for which he was writing), then I have translated, *tout court,* "the stiff-limbed god Priapus."[42] Cohen's rendering, "the stiff garden-god,"[43] seems to me to shirk the translator's responsibility—that is, the obligation to transmit a meaningful text, and not simply some replication of the original's mere *words.* "The stiff garden-god" is "correct," for whatever mere lexical correctness is worth. But it is not useful and, to my mind, it is poor translation. It is, to be sure, what we might by this point take to calling Penguin-consistent, just as Le Clerq's rendering is true to his approach: "the erect god of gardens, Priapus."[44] I think Le Clerq goes too far, but his approach comes a good deal closer to the original than does Cohen's, for all that in lexical accuracy Le Clerq falls far short. He at least understands the all-important truth that literature is not merely an assemblage of words, but of words organized into something more than words, with shape and structure and tone and, in the end, with the meaning that comes from all its various parts having been thus assembled. When Cohen translates the chapter heading, "Comment Panurge . . . mangeoit son bled en herbe" (*Tiers Livre,* chap. 2), as "How Panurge . . . ate his Wheat in the Blade,"[45] he has in a sense not translated

41. Trans. Cohen, 386; Urquhart and Le Motteux, vol. 2, 555, trans. Le Clerq, 421. Though the original does not say where Paul may be found to have said what he is quoted as saying, Le Clerq makes Rabelais explain himself in careful bibliographical detail: "when he [Paul] stated in 1 *Corinthians,* VII, 29." In these matters, as indeed in many others, every solution creates a problem.

42. Trans. Raffel, 314.

43. Trans. Cohen, 363.

44. Trans. Le Clerq, 393.

45. Trans. Cohen, 292.

at all, for the string of words Cohen has here produced means, as I have noted earlier, nothing, and what the French idiomatic expression is intended to convey (*bled* being modern French *blé*) is in fact that Panurge, a notorious spendthrift, "spent his money before he got it."

Similarly, except for some principal names that have passed into common use, or are so familiar to readers that they cannot be changed, I have preferred to translate (from Greek, French, or whatever language Rabelais employs) these proper nouns into meaningful ones. In *Gargantua,* chap. 33, for example, when King Picrochole receives three of his loyal subjects, and Rabelais writes "comparurent devant Picrochole les ducs de Menuail, comte Spadassin et captaine Merdaille," I have translated the underlings' mocking names but not the equally mocking one assigned to the king (though the first time it is used, I *have* informed my readers that Picrochole signifies a man whose character is bitter and bile-ridden): "The duke of Slobdom, together with Count Boastwell and Captain Shitface, came to Picrochole."[46] If in the same chapter Rabelais writes "Alexandre Macedo" ("Alexander of Macedon"), I have changed the name to conform to modern usage, "Alexander the Great."[47] If in chapter 36 of the same book Rabelais tells us of a horse, trained "selon le doctrine de Aelian" ("according to Aelian's doctrines/ideas"), I have lightly expanded my translation to read "according to the methods set out by Aelian in *De natura animalium,* On the Nature of Animals."[48] Historical references have frequently been handled in the same way— that is, not copiously and certainly not fully explained, but sufficiently clarified so that the reader who wants to know more can be guided in his hunt, and the reader (most readers) who will not take that trouble need not be bothered: there is enough already on the page to at least orient him. Cohen translates, "by Aelian's method,"[49] and as I have said I do not think that sufficiently helpful.

But the truest test (or perhaps the final graveyard) of my approach comes in the seventh chapter of *Pantagruel,* in which Rabelais details for our delectation the "beaux livres de la librairie de Sainct Victor" ("the lovely books in Saint Victor's Library"). He must have rolled in the aisles, writing this mock bibliography; his contemporaries seem to have similarly laughed themselves silly. But what is the modern reader to think, confronted with page after page of book titles like (I give the bare beginning of a closely printed seven-page list that took literally weeks to more or less translate):

46. Trans. Raffel, 78.
47. Ibid.
48. Ibid., 86.
49. Trans. Cohen, 118.

Bigua Salutis
Bragueta juris
Pantofla Decretorum
Malogranatum vitiorum
Le Peloton théologie
Le Vistempenard des Prescheurs, composé par Turelupin
Le Couillebarine des Preux
Les Hanebanes des evesques.

If you do not find that these titles conduce to instant hilarity, you are in the same position as 99.999999 percent of modern readers.

What then is the translator to do? Cohen has chosen, as I have, to reproduce the Latin, when a title is in Latin in the original, and to list the English alongside; titles originally in French are given only in English. But I have also chosen at least to try to make these renderings funny, and in the spirit (if not always quite the letter) of the original—for otherwise what is the point to inflicting this long long list on the reader? Without repeating the Latin, here then are Cohen's and my renderings of these titles, side by side:

Cohen	*Raffel*
The Props of Salvation	Riding High on Salvation
The Codpiece of the Law	The Law's Codpiece
The Slipper of the Decretals	Soft Slippers and Hard Decrees
The Pomegranate of Vice	How to Blow Up Vice
The Thread-ball of Theology	Theology's Tennis Ball
The Long Broom of Preachers, composed by Turlupin	The Preacher's Featherduster, written by a bum
The Elephantine Testicle of the Valiant	Heroes' Elephant Balls
The Henbane of the Bishops[50]	Bishops' Antidotes for Aphrodisiacs[51]

Without going into close analysis of these two translations, I think— I certainly hope—that if one seems wittier than the other, even perhaps funny after a fashion, it is my rendition rather than Cohen's which deserves the nod. Le Clerq's approach not only gives the Latin, but also invents a bit of Latin, as in "*Ars Theologiae,* The Arse of Theology," which he substitutes for the fifth item on the list, given

50. Ibid., 187.
51. Trans. Raffel, 151.

in the original text only in French.[52] For the rest, his renderings, though more apt than Cohen's (it is I think not difficult to surpass Cohen, here and elsewhere), to my mind are on the whole neither funnier nor less funny than mine:

> The Tumbril of Salvation
> The Codpiece of the Law
> The Slippers of the Decretals
> The Pomegranate of Vice
> The Arse of Theology
> The Preacher's Dinglescrew by Turlupin
> The Lush Ballock of Heroes
> The Henbane of Bishops[53]

There is a kind of inspired madness to "The Preacher's Dinglescrew." It does not come close to "translating" the French, but it is emphatically Rabelaisian. I do not share Le Clerq's general approach to the translation of prose, though I think it plainly applicable to the translation of poetry. But I rather envy him such coinages: they *ought* to be by Rabelais, even though they are not.

But for the translator the hardest pages of all, I suspect, are those which Rabelais clearly intended to be non-sense. The rollicking scatological pages, especially the excremental explosion at the end of the *Quart Livre,* present only minor problems, on the order of: How many ways can one find to say "shit" in English? Rabelais finds sixteen in French; it is just barely possible for the translator to match him.

> Ha, ha, ha! Houay! Que diable est cecy? Appelez-vous cecy foyre, bren, crottes, merde, fiant, déjection, matière fécale, excrément, repaire, laisse, esmeut, fumée, estront, scybale ou spyrathe? C'est, croy-je, sapphran d'Hibernie. Ho, ho, hie! C'est sapphran d'Hibernie! Sela! Beuvons! (*Quart Livre,* chap. 67)

> Ha, ha, ha! Hooray!! What the devil is this, anyway? Do you call this stuff right here diarrhea, crap, dung, shit, turds, bowel leavings, fecal matter, excrement, ordure, droppings, bird lime, slop, offal, dried-up diarrhea, or goat shit? Ho, ho, hey! It's Spanish saffron, by God! Damned right! So let's drink![54]

52. Trans. Le Clerq, 185; *Pantagruel,* ed. V. L. Saulnier (Geneva, 1965), 37.
53. Trans. Le Clerq, 185.
54. Trans. Raffel, 522.

Yet this is relatively simple, a matter of mere lexicon; the words are piled up like so much ordure, one on top of the other. Even the Penguin translator cannot do too much damage, given these limitations:

> Ha, ha, ha! But, ho! What the devil's this? Do you call it shit, turds, crots, ordure, deposit, fecal matter, excrement, droppings, fumets, motion, dung, stronts, scybale, or pyrathe? It's saffron from Ireland,[55] that's what I think it is. Ho, ho, ho! Saffron from Ireland! It is indeed. Let's have a drink.[56]

"Crots" is not a word in my own lexicon, nor can I find it in G. N. Garmonsway's *Penguin English Dictionary*, which records twentieth-century British usage. Nor is it in the *OED* or the Merriam-Webster *Unabridged Dictionary*, 2d ed. I do however find it in Eric Partridge, *A Dictionary of Slang and Unconventional English*, where it is explained as "schoolboy" slang, vintage "ca. 1935."[57] The presence of one such intrusion creates no significant difficulty—but "fumets"? "stronts"? "scybale"? "spyrathe"? Would a translator seriously interested in communicating the sense of his scatalogical author rely on this sort of vocabulary? Or intrude into this dung-drenched list a word like "motion"?

In any event, lexical meaning is almost the only thing at issue in such wonderfully excremental eruptions: what may seem difficult to the squeamish is in fact not terribly difficult at all. But things are very different in the non-sense passages, where neither lexical nor any other sense can possibly be of concern (or even be a point of reference for the struggling translator). In passages like that just discussed, the translator is not confronted with deviant syntactic structure. Clauses do not slip and slide in the hard-blowing rhetorical breeze, the tumbling incoherencies do not confuse, the constantly deceptive appearance of rationality does not interfere—as they do when "le seigneur de Humevesne" ("My Lord Fartsniffer") begins his juridical pleading:

> Monsieur et Messieurs, si l'iniquité des hommes estoit aussi facilement veue en jugement catégoricque comme on congnoist

55. Lexically possibly accurate: *sapphran d'Hibernie* = "saffron from Ireland" according to some editors. But Robert Marichal, editor of the Droz edition, says that *Hibernie* = *Espagne* (Spain), and explains that the reference is to "saffran de qualité médiocre." *Le Quart Livre*, Droz ed., 318. The editors of the bilingual Editions de Seuil edition agree with Marichal, and for the same reason: "Le saffran d'Espagne était de qualité inférieure." Rabelais, *Oeuvres Complètes* (Paris: Editions du Seuil, 1973), 766b n.29.

56. Trans. Cohen, 597.

57. Eighth ed. (New York: Macmillan, 1984), 273a.

mousches en laict, le monde, quatre beufz, ne seroit tant mangé
de ratz comme il est, et seroient aureilles maintes sur terre qui
en ont esté rongées trop laschement: car, —combien que tout ce
que a dit partie adverse soit de dumet bien vray quand à la lettre
et histoire du *factum*—toutesfoys, Messieurs, la finesse, la tricherie,
les petitz hanicrochements sont cachéz soubz le pot aux roses.
(*Pantagruel,* chap. 12)[58]

Rabelais's artfulness, here, is primarily stylistic rather than baldly lexical,
and it is conveyed—as part one of this book argues it would be—via a
carefully constructed simulacrum of subtle, legal argument, which is in
turn expressed by means of a close, harmonious aping of the syntactic
movement of such argument. To get the *words* largely correct but at the
same time ignore any part of this rhythmical, structural "meaning," is to
lose much of what the original contains. Here are, first, my own translation of this paragraph and then Cohen's:

My dear sir, and gentlemen all: if the evil that men do were as
readily visible, and could be as conveniently and categorically
catalogued, as the flies one sees in milk, the entire world—by the
four great oxen that stand at each of its corners!—would not be
eaten up by rats as, demonstrably, it now is, and there would
be many, many ears here on this earth that would not be so
disastrously and cowardly gnawed as now they most certainly
are. Because, although every word that my opponent has said
may be goose-featherly true, according to the letter and the
precise history of the *factum,* the facts in the case before you,
nevertheless, gentlemen, the subtleties, the lies, all the little
snags and difficulties are hidden under the pot of roses.[59]

My lord and gentlemen, if the iniquity of men were as easily seen
in categorical judgment as one detects flies in milk, the world—by
the four oxen!—would not be so rat-eaten as it is, and there
would be many ears on earth that have been too disgracefully

58. I here follow Boulenger's *Pléiade* edition, as well as that published by Editions du
Seuil, both of which follow the 1542 edition, rather than V. L. Saulnier's Droz text, which is
concerned, for historical reasons, to show what was in *Pantagruel* when it first appeared, in
1532. Saulnier's "Note sur le texte," however, freely concedes that the 1542 edition "doit
être considérée comme l'édition 'définitive' " ("must be considered the 'definitive' edition"),
adding quite accurately that the later and much altered version "est le texte suivi par
l'édition magistrale, comme par toutes les éditions modernes" ("is the text followed by the
authoritative/master edition, and also by all modern editions"). Saulnier, 51.

59. Trans. Raffel, 171.

nibbled away. For, although everything that the opposing party
has said is of down, quite true, as to the letter and history of the
factum, nevertheless, gentlemen, the subtleties, the trickeries,
the little catches are hidden under the rose pot.[60]

Fartsniffer's speech, like much of Lewis Carroll's writing, cannot be
parsed, in the usual meaning of the term. (Cohen, by the way, translates
the character's name "Suckfizzle," and since in British usage "fizzle"
apparently means, as a noun, the act of petering/fizzling out, I think it fair
to classify this translation, too, as bowdlerization.[61]) But the movement
of Fartsniffer's rhetoric, its calmly unwinding periods, combined with its
utter insanity, can make us sense, feel, and thus appreciate the effectiveness
of Rabelais's "parodie du galimatias juridique de l'époque"[62] ("parody of
the grandiloquent nonsense of the time's legal language"), even though the
words as words mean nothing. That is, in a sense we apprehend this
sort of thing nonverbally—not through what the words mean, but in
contrast to what they might mean, when spoken in this way, if, that is,
they meant anything. The key phrase, however, remains "when spoken in
this way": again, the *manner* of Fartsniffer's speech is crucial, not the matter.
Cohen's translation, alas, does not unroll so much as it proceeds, as it
merely occurs. The translation is not quite hurried, but neither is it so
ridiculously stately, so elaborately pompous, as Rabelais requires it to be
to achieve the effect he wants. It is not coincidental that Cohen's version
employs a total of 91 words, and mine, intent on reproducing Rabelais's
decorous, mindless verbosity, employs a total of 137. In the interests of
making as little claim upon the reader's attention as possible, Cohen uses
eleven commas; in trying to rub the reader's nose in this pseudo-legal
farrago (another meaning of *galimatias*), as Rabelais most certainly does,
I use sixteen, or a full 50 percent more. The reader *must* be made aware
of the author's designs; to shield the reader from those designs, instead of
revealing them to him, is not to translate but to betray the original. Note
how Cohen for the most part takes the syntactic *sequence* of the original
as his guide, blandly reproducing only what follows after what in the
French, rather than trying to reproduce its movement and flow. Nor does
he help the reader who may be puzzled by the four oxen by whom
Fartsniffer suddenly swears, or the reader who is not entirely sure just

60. Trans. Cohen, 208.
61. Since (a) *hume,* the first part of the litigant's name, means "to sniff," and *vesne*
probably means "stink," (b) the other litigant's name is an unequivocal *Baisecul,* meaning
"kiss my ass," and (c) Rabelais is Rabelais, my translation seems accurate. But as with much
else in Rabelais, one cannot be absolutely certain.
62. Sainéan, vol. 2, 383.

what *factum* is supposed to mean. Nor does Cohen rise to the challenge of an assertion said to be "de dumet bien vray" ("surely fluffy-down true"), but translates this charmingly evocative phrase blandly, flatly, as "of down, quite true." Though Rabelais rises to all occasions, and to all baits, Cohen as a matter of Penguin policy rises to none.

Nor am I, for all that I may seem to be, flogging a dead horse: because of the size of Penguin's list, the relatively low unit cost of each title, the worldwide distribution, and the extensive advertising support given by the publisher, paperback volumes in the Penguin Classics series, in which Cohen's translation appears, tend to be the translations of choice wherever English is spoken and/or taught. So determinedly leveling (read "destructive") an editorial policy as Penguin seems to employ, accordingly, is the very farthest thing from a dead or a merely academic issue. Indeed, it is all too live, and all too pressing.

Fartsniffer's speech, finally, emphasizes the importance of yet another serious but insufficiently understood aspect of translating Rabelais, and that is the handling of dialogue. An extraordinary proportion of the book is in fact written in dialogue form; chapter 5 of *Gargantua,* "Les propos des bien yvres" ("The talk/chatter/conversation of the good-and-drunk"), is perhaps the most striking example. Here, Rabelais does not bother to tell us who is saying what to whom, because what matters is what is being said, not who happens to be saying it. We are never even told who *could* be saying what to whom: this is a speech tapestry woven by entirely anonymous speakers—or almost entirely anonymous: the highly particularized language of some participants indicates at least what professions or sexes they belong to. They are all at a wedding, and seated around a long, festive table; they are celebrating exactly as Rabelais liked best to see people celebrate, namely, by tippling freely; and their conversation is uproariously funny, as well as deeply revealing. I can quote only a small part of this chapter-long, beautifully handled counterpoint:

> —Par my fy, ma commère, je ne peuz entrer en bette.
> —Vous estex morfondue, m'amie?
> —Voire.
> —Ventre sainct Quenet! parlons de boire.
> —Je ne bois que à mes heures, comme la mulle du pape.
> —Je ne boy que en mon brévaire, comme un beau père guardian.
> —Qui feut premier, soif ou beuverye?
> —Soif, car qui eust beu sans soif durant le temps de innocence?
> —Beuverye, car *privatio presupponit habitum.* Je suis clerc. *Foecundi calices quem non fecere disertum?*
> —Nous aultres innocens ne beuvons que trop sans soif.

Truncating so jolly a colloquy is truly a shame, to use no stronger word, but this book does not propose to rival the length of Rabelais's. We would expect seventeenth-century translators to handle such alcoholic exuberance with practiced ease: here then is the Urquhart and Le Motteux version of this passage:

—By my figgins, godmother, I cannot as yet enter in the humour of being merry, nor drink so currently as I would.

—You have catched a cold, gammer.

—Yea forsooth, sir.

—By the belly of Saint Buff! let us talk of our drink.

—I never drink but at my hours, like the pope's mule. [footnote]

—And I never drink but in my breviary, like a fair father guardian. [footnote]

—Which was first, thirst or drinking?

—Thirst, for who in the time of innocence would have drunk without being athirst?

—Nay, sir, it was drinking; for *privatio praesupponit habitum.* [footnote] I am learned, you see. *Foecundi calices quem non fecere disertum?*

—We poor innocents drink but too much without thirst.[63]

What we find, surprisingly, is that Rabelais's first English translators have a number of serious deficiences: quite apart from the distinctly outmoded speech they employ, they do not quite seem either fully to understand the passage or to grasp the difference between written and spoken English. The French, for example, says "Qui feut premier, soif ou beuverye?" and if we take this quite literally (as of course we cannot), it does indeed seem to say "Which was first, thirst or drinking?" But *feut* is clearly idiomatic here; the sentence has to be translated "Which *came* first?" "Entrer en bette" is similarly idiomatic, signifying "manage it." Urquhart and Le Motteux thrash mightily, producing the verbose, imprecise, and unspeechlike "enter in the humour of being merry, nor drink so currently as I would." Fourteen floundering words instead of three French ones is a bad exchange. The feminine form, *amie,* indicates that the person being spoken to, who is also the person saying "By my figgins," is female; *commère* means "gossip, drinking partner." "Godmother" seems to be intended as a translation of *commère.* But if "godmother" is a shaky rendering, "parlons de boire" as "let us talk of our drink" is an impossible one: no one at any time, on either side of the Atlantic, has ever spoken in

63. Trans. Urquhart and Le Motteux, vol. 1, 209.

such cripplingly stilted style. Further, without consulting the footnote (which makes matters clear), it is hard to know what is meant by "drink but in my breviary," Urquhart and Le Motteux's rendering of "ne boy que en mon brévaire." Again, without consulting the editors' footnote "A fair father guardian" is similarly obscure as a translation for "un beau père guardian." The linguistic puzzle is hardly an insoluble one—as Jacques Boulenger points out, "Il existait des flacons en forme de bréviaires" ("There used to be flasks shaped like prayer books")[64]—but these are things that need, if at all possible, to be clear in the text proper. In short, Urquhart and Le Motteux, though their translation is still of considerable interest, cannot substitute for a clear modern version. It is all too plain that, writing when they did, they do not share our modern belief that Rabelais, like any great writer, generally knew what he was talking about and, when he chose to write nonsense, made it clear what he was doing.

> "Upon my word, gammer my darling, I can't feel my way into drinking!"
> "You've taken cold, my sweet."
> "Ay, so I have, I'm thinking."
> "By the belly of Bachus! Let's talk about drinking!"
> "I only drink at my hours; capricious, I am, like the Pope's mule."
> "Pass me that flask shaped like a breviary; I'll drink no other wine; a pious man, I; I'll have breviary wine, ay, like a f-f-fine F-f-franciscan F-f-father S-s-s-s-superior."
> "Which came first: thirst or drinking?"
> "Thirst came first. Who would have thought of drinking without being thirsty, in the age of innocence?"
> "Drink came first, for *privatio presupponit habitum,* says the law: privation of something presupposes being accustomed to it. A clerk, I. *'Foecundi calices quem non fecere disertum'* Horace put it aptly: the cups of the talkative, but not the eloquent!"
> "The age of innocence, you said? We poor innocents drink all too much without being thirsty!"[65]

This is clearly better, though it is both wordy and, I suspect, rather too insistently uproarious; Rabelais has a finer touch than this translation would indicate. Having explained the flask-shaped-like-a-prayerbook reference, Le Clerq proceeds to make the point over and over: the flask is "shaped like a breviary"; he'll "drink no other wine" (a joke: only sancti-

64. Boulenger, ed., *Oeuvres complètes,* 16 n.10.
65. Trans. Le Clerq, 16–17.

fied alcohol goes down this deeply religious gullet); and "I'll have breviary wine." And if the translator hadn't already laid it on too thickly, he
ends with a burst of purportedly humorous stuttering that is entirely his
own invention, and is I'm afraid not notably funny. Indeed, though the
French gets the job done in a sparse twelve words, Le Clerq's translation
expands this to twenty-eight. Rabelais is word-besotted, to be sure. But
the decision to say the same thing three times over is one that must be
left to him, for not only is he the author but he is also a full-fledged
Humanist, a man of the Renaissance, and not a man of the Middle Ages.
That is, he is well acquainted with *mensura* ("limit, extent, degree,
measure"). He is not a man of restraint—but that is another issue entirely.
When Rabelais breaks with *mensura,* we must concede him the knowledge that he is doing so: our job as translators is to understand why, not
to substitute our judgment for his. He must be allowed to break whatever
rules *he* chooses, as and when he chooses.

> —God bless me, my dear, I can't get my gullet working.—You've
> caught a chill, old girl.—You're right.—By St Quenet's guts, let's
> talk of drink.—I only drink at my own times, like the Pope's
> mule.—And I only drink from my breviary flask [footnote], like a
> good Father Superior.—Which came first, drinking or thirst?—
> Thirst. For who could have drunk without a thirst in the time
> of innocence?—Drinking, for *privatio praesupponit habitum.*
> [footnote] I'm a Latinist. *Foecundi calices quem no fecere
> disertum?* [footnote] We poor innocents drink only too much
> with no thirst.[66]

Again, the Penguin translation is distinguished in only two respects: it
is rhetorically and rhythmically flat, and it includes sentences either
unidiomatic or difficult to stay with across their entire length. "Let's talk
of drink" is no better than Urquhart and Le Motteux's "Let us talk of our
drink." The structure of "We poor innocents drink only too much with no
thirst" resembles nothing so much as a series of railroad cars: as so often
in Cohen's graceless prose, the words are clamped together without
regard for the most obvious considerations of prose euphony. Rabelais, as
I and many others before me have said, is a master stylist. Cohen is no
stylist at all.

> "Oops, my dear (burped a woman): I can't get it down."
> "My love, are you too cold?"

66. Trans. Cohen, 48-49.

"It looks like it."

"By Saint Quenet's belly, let's talk about drinking."

"I only drink when church bells ring—or a papal bull bellows."

"Me, I only drink when my prayer book says so—just like a good and proper abbot."

"Which came first—thirst or drinking?"

"Thirst. How could you drink if you weren't thirsty, back in the days when we were all innocent?"

"No, drinking. Because *privatio presupponit habitum:* 'if there's something missing, then there's got to be something that used to be there.' Me, I'm a scholar. *Foecundi calices quem non fecere disertum?* 'Is there anyone who hasn't been turned into an orator by having his glass continually refilled?'—as Horace puts it."

"The rest of us innocents drink quite enough, even without being thirsty."[67]

I do not like the translation of "Voire": at the time, I thought the necessary briskness was carried by "It looks like it." I was wrong and will ask the publisher to change the rendering, in the next printing, to "Damned right." But I stand by the rest of the translation, which I think is both better English and a better representation of Rabelais's French than anything in print. I should add, I think, that the identification of "breviary" and "flask" is possible but not definite: there *were* such objects, but whether or not Rabelais is here referring to them remains uncertain. Since the previous speaker has brought in the sounding of church *heures,* which I have translated as "church bells," and proceeds to also make a relatively obscure joke that I have turned into a "papal bull" bellowing, it seems sensible to link the next speaker's reference to "mon brévaire" ("my prayer book") to what the person just before him has been saying. That, as I understand both this passage and this author, is what Rabelais meant to do.

67. Trans. Raffel, 16-17.

6

Translating Cervantes

Vladimir Nabokov, whose critical opinions tend to be both absolute and absolutely untrustworthy, did not think much of *Don Quijote.* If I do not misread his words, he could and did read the novel only in translation, which explains a good deal, for virtually all the translations into English have been at best (in Nabokov's words) only "more or less adequate,"[1] and at worst execrable. It is risky, not to say foolhardy, so to evaluate what all native speakers of Spanish and many others beside have for centuries called the greatest novel ever written.[2] But Nabokov wrote not as a critic, with the responsibilities and also with the relative humility of the scholar, but as a practicing novelist of unlimited ambition and boundless arrogance. It seems to have been a professional obligation for him to like very little that others (except Russians, and by no means all of them) had written: there would of course be more room at the top, where he placed himself, if fewer rivals were left to occupy those heights. "The [emigré Russian] author that interested me most," he records in a memoir, *Speak Memory,* "was naturally Sirin. . . . Among the young writers produced in

1. Vladimir Nabokov, *Lectures on Don Quixote* (New York: Harcourt Brace Jovanovich, 1983), 10.
2. As will be abundantly clear in a moment, I am one of the "many others."

exile he turned out to be the only major one."[3] Sirin was of course Nabokov's own pseudonym, under which he published, in Russian, his first novels. All of Nabokov's considered judgments, accordingly, have most emphatically to be considered in the light of who framed them, and why:

> Don Quixote has been called the greatest novel ever written. This, of course, is nonsense. As a matter of fact, it is not even one of the greatest novels of the world . . . the book lives and will live through the sheer vitality that Cervantes has injected into the main character of a very patchy haphazard tale, which is saved from falling apart only by its creator's wonderful artistic intuition that has his Don Quixote go into action at the right moments of the story.[4]

It may not seem of any particular significance in a discussion focused on translating Don Quijote, to show how easy it would be for so brilliant a writer as Vladimir Nabokov, reading Cervantes' book only in English translation, to be so incredibly wrong about the greatest novel ever written. Nabokov's motivations are indeed of no relevance here, but since the translations may well have been the source for his error, and for similarly flagrant misjudgments by others both living and dead, the inadequacies of those translations are extraordinarily relevant.

Let me begin with a deceptively simple-looking metaphor, in chapter 7 of Don Quijote's second volume. The addled knight's housekeeper, terrified that he is going to "break out" and "go off again"—that is, ride away on Rocinante, Sancho Panza trailing after, seeking resplendent adventures— runs to seek help from a new friend, a recent and very cocksure university graduate, Samson Carrasco. In describing how her master appeared on returning home from earlier adventures, she describes him as having looked "flaco, amarillo, los ojos hundidos en los últimos camaranchones del celebro" ("weak/thin, yellow, his eyes sunk/drowned/merged in the last/furthest/final attic/loft of his skull/brain"). Although there is in British usage an excellent and fairly exact translation for at least the central meaning of the word camaranchón (again, meaning a kind of

3. Vladimir Nabokov, Speak Memory (New York: Grosset & Dunlop, 1951), 216.

4. Nabokov, Lectures, 27-28. As Edmund Wilson, a very great and almost awesomely responsible critic, wrote to Nabokov, in late 1946, "You and I . . . differ completely, not only about Malraux [N. had criticized him for being, among other things, humorless], but also about Dostoevsky, Greek drama, Lenin, Freud, and a lot of other things." Edmund Wilson, Letters on Literature and Politics, 1912-1972, ed. Elena Wilson (New York: Farrar, Straus & Giroux, 1977), 444.

attic storeroom; the British term is "lumber room," and it has no true equivalent in American usage), the Penguin Classics British translator, once again Mr. J. M. Cohen, chooses to omit the metaphor completely. He translates, that is, as though the Spanish read, quite straightforwardly, "los ojos hundidos en el celebro" ("his eyes sunk right into his skull").[5] This sort of determined leveling is, as we have seen, typical of his work, and of the approach taken by virtually all the translators in the Penguin Classics series—not that this is quite so bad a rendering as some Penguin translations we have examined. All the same, there is a specific, imaginative force to "los ojos hundidos en *los últimos camaranchones* del celebro" which simply is not present in the more familiar, predictable "los ojos hundidos en el celebro." Finding an exact English-language equivalent is of course a genuine difficulty: even "lumber room" is not exact, because although it means "a room where unused furniture is kept,"[6] that room can be anywhere, on any floor. Not only does "lumber room" have no necessary connection to an "attic" room, but a *camaranchón* is quite specifically in the attic, and this particular *camaranchón* is "en los *últimos* camaranchones" ("*the very last* of all the *camaranchones,*" or, in short, "all the way up in the attic"). That highly specific location further complicates the translator's task, if he is to carry over the full sense and flavor of the original—and faced with such a degree of difficulty we may, along with virtually all translators of *Don Quijote,* stop and ask ourselves: Is this metaphor really worth all the trouble? Is it in fact important enough so that the translator needs to wrestle with it, rather than simply cutting the Gordian Knot and getting on with his business? The answer, it seems to me, is the key to really translating Cervantes' novel, and though the answer given by earlier translators has been a consistent no, it is not worth it at all, we have other fish to fry, I would insist that if Cervantes thought the metaphor important enough to put into his masterpiece, the translator had damned well better find it of equal importance. Working directly in Spanish, a language of peculiarly subtle nature, almost indeed a language more of indirection than of forthright statement,[7] Cervantes quite likely did not have to wrestle with the formulation of his metaphor. But what has that got to do with

5. Miguel de Cervantes Saavedra, *Don Quixote,* trans. J. M. Cohen (Harmondsworth: Penguin, 1950), 508. Although *Don Quixote* is the original spelling of the novel's title, the early seventeenth-century pronunciation, "kee-shoat-ey," is closer to the sound of the modern Spanish *Quijote,* "kee-xot-ey," than is the sound of the modern English *Quixote,* "kwiks-ot." (I am indebted to Professor Michael McGaha for clarification of these matters.) And since the novel is and has been for years passionately read and adored by millions as *Don Quijote,* that is the title given it by my translation.

6. *Penguin English Dictionary,* 430a.

7. I will amplify this observation in a moment.

the translator, who may not have the advantage of working in Spanish, but who ought not to forget that he, alas, is not Cervantes. If Miguel de Cervantes Saavedra wanted his reader to see Don Quijote's emaciation in these exact terms, then that is what the translator is required to do. As both a translator and a critic of translators I can be, and I have been, less insistent about the absolute primacy of the original, in dealing with the translation of lesser authors. But the greatest novel ever written cannot be translated like any ordinary book: the more the writer of such a book is capable of, the more his or her translator is obliged to do.

Samuel Putnam's translation, "His eyes were deep-sunken in his head,"[8] is in part less bland: "deep-sunken" is livelier than "sunk," and therefore evokes somewhat more of the energy and strength of the original. But not only does Putnam's version similarly omit the metaphor, but it still further compromises Cervantes' meaning by translating *celebro* (skull, brain) as "head." The Spanish word for "head" is *cabeza,* a word with which Cervantes is of course very familiar. A man's "head" is what sits on his neck; it comes complete with eyes, nose, ears, hair, and the like. When we strip away these anatomical appurtenances, we come to the "skull." There is of course a definite relationship between "head" and "skull"; there are special contexts (medical, legal) in which the two words can be used more or less interchangeably. But in the usual parlance employed in a novel the words are quite unlike: a character who finds a human "skull" has clearly found something different from, though arguably no less gruesome than, a human "head." Again, Cervantes knows the difference, and has chosen "skull," not "head." I do not think his translator has any choice at all.

Another translator, Walter Starkie—Irish, rather than English—translates the phrase as "with his eyes deep sunk in the recesses of his skull."[9] This is still better than Putnam's rendering, because "recesses" at least echoes, even if it does not translate, the metaphor. But "better," as I have said, is still not good enough, not for *Don Quijote.* Omission of the metaphor will not do.

John Ormsby's British translation, published in 1885, has been revised by two Americans, Joseph R. Jones and Kenneth Douglas. It is a dogged rendering, somewhat improved by being lightly modernized; it is generally reasonably close to the word meanings of the original, though as I

8. Miguel de Cervantes Saavedra, *Don Quixote,* trans. Samuel Putnam (New York: Viking, 1949; reprint, *The Portable Cervantes,* New York: Viking, 1951), 428.

9. Miguel de Cervantes Saavedra, trans. Walter Starkie, *Don Quixote* (London: Macmillan, 1957; reprint, New York: Signet, 1964), 570. Professor Jones, one of the revisers of the Ormsby translation, indicates that Starkie's translation too is a revision of Ormsby, rather than, as claimed, a new translation. (See the note to page ix of the translation cited at note 10 herein.)

have indicated mere verbal "meaning" is emphatically not all the meaning a text possesses, and Ormsby frequently seems so closed to all other meanings that it would be hard to understand, without access to the Spanish, why Cervantes' characters are saying and doing what he tells us they are up to. Those who already know the Spanish can more readily relate to this translation. But those who know only English will find it, as a host of university students can testify, unbearably dull. Messrs Ormsby, Jones, and Douglas translate the snippet here at issue "with his eyes sunk deep into his skull."[10] This is more or less on a par with the flat, conventional, and low-keyed Penguin rendering: it is not "wrong," but neither is it "right." Omission of a key metaphor is omission of a key metaphor; leveling is leveling; and this sort of thing is simply not how *Don Quijote* should be translated. In fact, I would argue that, with this approach, what *is* translated is so little of the original as to be, essentially, not a translation at all, but a kind of low-level paraphrase. No one reading this kind of thing should be encouraged to think he has been reading *Don Quijote.*

Finally, Tobias Smollett (or whatever eighteenth-century British person or persons did the work to which Smollett affixed his name) translates our snippet with a bright, cavalier hand: "his eyes sunk into the very lowest pit of his brain."[11] All the same, reversing the direction permits Smollett (or his surrogate) to at least give his readers *a* metaphorical description. Nor is the metaphor he creates by his reversal quite so cavalier as it may seem: "sunk into the very lowest *pit*" is in fact an imaginative touch, bringing across quite a lot of the original, and certainly a great deal more than is transmitted by any of the other versions. To be sure, "pit" carries associations that have nothing to do with *un camaranchón.* Seeing an object in the mirror, or standing an object on its head, are surely not preferred methods of translation. And Cervantes certainly deserves the best translation he can receive. But Smollett's rendering seems to me the most adequate of an essentially inadequate lot.

I would not have translated *Don Quijote,* had I found any of the extant translations satisfactory. To that extent, every new translator of a classic book makes a distinctly egocentric claim. Nor would I have completed my translation, or allowed it to see print, if I did not think it in fact a better version than anything that has been available in English—though the very first words of my prefatory "Translator's Note" say bluntly that

10. Miguel de Cervantes Saavedra, *Don Quixote,* trans. John Ormsby, rev. J. R. Jones and Kenneth Douglas (New York: Norton, 1981), 457. I shall refer to this translation as "OJD."

11. Miguel de Cervantes Saavedra, *The Adventures of Don Quixote de la Mancha,* trans. Tobias Smollett (1755; reprint, New York: Farrar, Straus & Giroux, 1986), 459.

"no one can reproduce Cervantes' style in English."[12] In any event, I was determined not to relinquish Cervantes' metaphor and, after I no longer remember how many experiments, finally came up with this version: "his eyes shrunk way up into the attic storerooms of his skull." Lacking a suitable English idiom, what I have done, essentially, is combine (or at least juxtapose) two native English terms, "attic" and "storerooms," thereby producing something comprehensible, more or less idiomatic (at least, not jarringly *un*idiomatic) and, most important, a translation significantly closer to what Cervantes actually meant and wrote than I believe any of my predecessors has been able (or has cared) to do. This alone probably would not have swayed Vladimir Nabokov; he was in general not a man who liked to change his opinions for any reason, bad or good. But perhaps a myriad such careful trackings of Cervantes' Spanish might have obliged him at least to modify his judgment of *Don Quijote*. Perhaps—though this is still less likely—so careful a translation might even have made him aware that Spanish as a language possesses subtleties and capabilities of which the non-Spanish speaking person cannot be aware. Nabokov knew this of Russian, and judged translations from that language accordingly. Remarkably few people seem to know this of Spanish, the formal regularity of which makes it relatively easy to speak, but the flavors and fragrances of which are not observable to casual visitors to a linguistic territory where even long acquaintance does not readily yield up the full bouquet.[13]

And when we even slightly expand our horizons, taking in a slightly longer passage, we can see perfectly clearly that Spanish in general, and *Don Quijote*'s Spanish in particular, can present us, in spaces no larger than a single sentence, with truly delicate and important meanings of many sorts, and on many levels. Failure to transmit these important aspects of Cervantes' novel—meanings so central to the overall meaning of the novel that not to transmit them in English amounts as I have said to substantial failure to actually translate the book—constitutes not casual error but serious betrayal. As should already be clear, and as will, I trust, become clearer still, all earlier translators of *Don Quijote* have been guilty, a thousand times over, of exactly such traitorous conduct.

12. My translation is to appear in 1995, in a Bantam paperback; the identity of the 1994 hardcover publisher is at this writing still under discussion. I therefore cannot give page citations. But volume and chapter numbers should be at least a workable if not an ideal substitute.

13. As cultural systems, constructed by discrete groups of human beings, all languages necessarily have their unique flavors and scents, just as other human-constructed systems do. Spanish architecture is not like French; Italian opera is not like German; British food is not like anything else on earth. As any and every French man or woman will readily tell you, *c'est la vie!*

The long section of the second volume, dealing with the duke and duchess of an unnamed and unidentifiable realm, is a clear case in point. If there is one part of the novel that, to my knowledge, "turns off" uninformed readers with no command of Spanish, it is these pages. As Englished by earlier translators, they seem dull, stagey, and—still worse— more or less pointless. Many readers begin to skip, not long after the novel introduces the duke and duchess; many who plod on find themselves powerfully disappointed. Is *this* really the greatest novel ever written, they ask plaintively?

Consider, to start with, the first point in the novel at which the duchess, destined (though the reader new to the book does not know it) to be a major character, speaks for herself.[14] We have seen her, initially, at a distance and from across a field, on horseback, with a falcon on her arm, and engaged in hunting; we glimpse her as she is first visible to Don Quijote and Sancho Panza. Then we have some typically jocose byplay between master and man, in the process of Don Quijote dispatching Sancho to greet this still unknown but obviously regal lady. After that, we have Sancho's florid speech of greeting, which is wonderfully ridiculous, drawn with such broad strokes that, almost no matter how it is translated, the humor survives. At this point the lady responds, and we can begin to fill in our portrait of her at first hand:

> "Por cierto, buen escudero," respondió la señora, "vos habéis dado la embajada vuestra con todas aquellas circunstancias que las tales embajadas piden. Levantaos del suelo; que escudero de tan grande caballero como es el de la Triste Figura, de quien ya tenemos acá mucha noticia, no es justo que esté de hinojos: levantaos, amigo, y decid a vuestro señor que venga mucho en hora buena a servirse de mí y del duque mi marido, en una casa de placer que aquí tenemos."

If Cervantes is the master, and if *Don Quijote* is the masterwork it is supposed to be, then this carefully prefaced and orchestrated speech ought to tell us a great deal. The prefatory matter has shown us Don Quijote and his squire acting and speaking in very familiar ways, the knight anxious to meet and to obtain the great lady's favor, Sancho equally impressed but, inevitably, unable to deliver a knightly message in properly knightly terms—and it is against this deft backdrop that the duchess's response has been set. It is a neatly crafted speech she gives, framed in exquisitely courteous language, which she, and we, know is

14. Vol. 2, chap. 30.

totally inappropriate to Sancho Panza's inspired, earnest ridiculousness. She says that Sancho has performed his errand exactly as all such errands must be performed; she asks him to rise, for the squire of such a knight as Don Quijote—and not only do *we* know what sort of knight he in fact is, but as she goes on to reveal, *she* knows too—ought not to be down on the ground on his knees. She has heard a great deal about Sancho's master, she says, and though she does not say how or where she has had "mucha noticia" ("a lot of news/ information") of our knight, we of course know that like so many people all over Spain she has been reading the sensationally popular first volume of the novel.[15] The duchess finishes her speech by giving Sancho a message to bring back to his master. Tell him, she says, that his coming is very opportune and he is most welcome ("en hora buena"). And why? So that she, and also her husband, the duke, can be taken advantage of ("a servirse") by Don Quijote, "in a pleasure home we maintain here," she concludes suggestively. We may at this point have some doubt exactly the kinds of pleasure she has in mind—though as far as Don Quijote is concerned, we know that the erotic sort is impossible: our knight does not *take* entertainment, but instead furnishes it. The duchess's final words clearly indicate that the noble pair are, as it were, "on vacation," having—or trying to have; there is a fascinating note of "exquisite boredom" about the duchess, here and hereafter, and her husband is portrayed as even more narrowly concerned with his own pleasure—a good time at a summer castle/vacation home they have in the vicinity.

What this speech conveys, plainly, is that the duchess, like any high-spirited aristocrat, and especially one on vacation, naturally loves a good time, especially at someone else's expense, and that as an aristocrat she fully intends to make sure that a good time is indeed what she has, given so ripe an opportunity as the appearance in the flesh of so superb a source of entertainment as Don Quijote. No concern for the personal interest or, except in a general sort of way, the well-being of her "victims" will (or, in her eyes, should) sway her: lesser folk have been put on earth, runs the code by which she has lived her entire life, for the express purpose of providing, in every way possible, for their betters. We can see at once that of course she has no intention of letting either Don Quijote or Sancho know what she, and by extension her pleasure-loving husband, are going to be up to. That would not only spoil the fun but would also involve the impossible admission that non-aristocrats have rights equal to those exercised by aristocrats. We as readers are by this point rubbing our hands in anticipatory delight, as—figuratively—she too is rubbing hers.

15. The first volume of *Don Quijote* appeared in 1605; after a long delay, a "sequel" not written by Cervantes appeared in 1614 and probably hastened the appearance of the second and final volume, in 1615.

Predictably, she is a superb actress. Watching her first appearance on stage, we are given abundant (and important) evidence of just how cool and collected she is.[16]

Here then is how the Penguin translation gives us this crucial first speech: as we are continually assured, none of us has more than one chance to make a first impression:

> "Indeed, good squire," answered the lady, "you have delivered your message with all the ceremony that such messages demand. Rise from the ground; for it is not right for the squire of so great a knight as he of the *Sad Countenance,* of whom we have already heard a great deal here, to remain on his knees. Rise, friend, and tell your master that he is most welcome to come and serve me and the Duke my husband, in a country house of ours near here."[17]

Where is the sly, gentle sarcasm? In Cervantes, the duchess gently lays it on, fooling Sancho but carefully not fooling us. But in this translation, she is forthright, almost businesslike: "Indeed, good squire ... " In the Spanish, she does not say anything about proper "ceremony," but only that Sancho has performed his task exactly as it ought to have been done—a delicately two-edged compliment readers find delightful and Sancho swallows whole. Cohen does not even permit the duchess any gracefulness of speech: "Rise from the ground," she says clunkingly, in phraseology just barely English, let alone graceful. The message to be returned to Don Quijote, in the original, is that he "venga mucho en hora buena" ("he comes very much at the right time"). Cohen utterly flattens (and indeed mistranslates) this into "he is most welcome to come," thus losing all the slyness. The regal residence, in the original, is "una casa de placer": without knowing much Spanish, and having in front of you only Cohen's translation, you would think that, since *casa* means "house," *placer* must therefore mean "country." But what *placer* actually means is "pleasure/comfort/joy," and what *casa de placer* means, accordingly, is "summer/holiday house/residence." Once again, Cohen has painstakingly leveled the original to the ground, transforming life-giving sparkle into life-depriving drabness, draining away sophisticated cunning in the interests of flat, humorless, humdrum communication, and of course destroying any possibility of letting the innocent reader become even faintly aware

16. In chapter 34, indeed, the duchess deliberately positions herself, on foot, to be the first to receive the charge of a deadly wild boar. Her husband obliges her to make an extremely unwilling retreat.

17. Trans. Cohen, 663.

of Cervantes' true meaning. Cohen's duchess is a petty bureaucrat, a minor civil servant, duly and mechanically acknowledging receipt of a message.

> "Good squire," replied the lady, "you've certainly delivered your message exactly as such messages are supposed to be delivered. Rise, for the squire of such a great knight as He of the Sad Face, of whom we have heard a great deal, should not be down on his knees—rise, my friend, and inform your lord that he comes most opportunely to be of service to me and to the duke, my husband, at a vacation home we maintain here.[18]

Having set out my own version, which I think comes a good deal closer to what Cervantes in fact wrote, let me add that, just as we speak, in English, of a stallion "servicing" a mare, so too there is a palpable whiff of sexuality about the Spanish verb *servirse,* which can mean "to court/woo," as well as "to seek the favor of." This is emphatically not the primary meaning of *servirse* here; it is at best a kind of subliminal association, almost more aura than clear intention—but it *is* there, nor does it fit badly with (a) the sort of character the duchess may well be, given her position and this speech, or (b) the duchess as she actually is, when we subsequently learn still more about her. Again, to trample all such possible meanings out of her opening speech is betrayal of a very serious order.

But it gets still worse. Without stopping to examine other manglings of this delicately written sally—for the other translators handle it much as Cohen does (though none of them quite have his peculiar and distinctive ability to betray both the Spanish and the English languages at the same time: "Rise from the ground" is in those terms a remarkable achievement)—let me take us two chapters further along, to another crucially important colloquy between Sancho and the duchess. What Cohen and, once more, all the earlier translators manage, in this passage, is to disinfect Cervantes' Spanish. That is, the sexual meanings are here not at all subliminal but perfectly clear: what earlier translators have accomplished is bowdlerization not in the interests of "safe sex" but in the name of "no sex."

> —No tengáis pena, amigo Sancho—dijo la duquesa—; que yo haré que mis doncellas os laven, y aun os metan en colada, si fuere menester.

18. Trans. Raffel.

—Con las barbas me contento—respondió Sancho—por ahora, a lo menos; que andando el tiempo, Dios dijo lo que será.

—Mirad, maestresala—dijo la duquesa—, lo que el buen Sancho pide, y cumplidle su voluntad al pie de la letra.[19]

This exchange comes just after the regal pair's serving maids, without the duke and duchess knowing they plan to do it, have used the after-dinner washing of guests' hands as a pretext for elaborately and publicly washing Don Quijote's beard, with great billows of rolling suds. The duke politely insists that his beard, too, must be washed; Sancho, amazed, has just observed that "un lavatorio de éstos antes es gusto que trabajo" ("a washing like this one just now is more pleasure/fun than labor/ punishment"). The serving maids are young and pretty. Don Quijote is as chaste as a rock, though now and then the rock stirs a bit—but Sancho, though safely married, has more than once indicated both that he is not immune to female seduction and that he cannot truly understand Don Quijote's immunity.

The key phrase is "aun os metan en colada" ("even get involved/mixed up with you"). Sancho, remember, has just remarked that the girls' behavior strikes him as more *gusto* than *trabajo,* and the duchess imme-diately replies that *pena* ("sorrow/penalty/punishment/grief") is exactly what he is *not* to experience: "No tengáis pena." Nor does she leave either Sancho or Cervantes' readers in doubt as to just why Sancho is to be feeling no pain: "Yo haré que mis doncellas os laven, y aun os metan en colada" ("I'll have my serving girls wash you, and even get involved/mixed up with you"). Sancho understands perfectly. "Con las barbas me contento" ("I'll be satisfied with just the beard"), he answers, adding at once, "por ahora, a lo menos" ("for now, at least"). Afterwards—well, we'll see what we'll see, he says. "Dios dijo lo que será" ("God only knows what will happen"). It is worth noting that what we in fact do see, not too long after, is that, with Sancho gone and Don Quijote visibly much depressed by his squire's absence, the duchess assures him that, among others, there are "doncellas ... en su casa, que le servirían a satisfación de su deseo" ("serving maids/girls/damsels in her house who would [future condi-tional tense] serve him so that his every desire would be satisfied"). Don Quijote asks simply to be left alone. But "no ha de ser así" ("it doesn't have to be like that"), insists the duchess, becoming even more explicit, "que le han de servir cuatro doncellas de las mías, hermosas como unas flores" ("because I've got four serving maids/damsels that you can have to serve you, each of them as lovely/beautiful as a flower"). Predictably,

19. Vol. 2, chap. 32.

Don Quijote declines, and squirms out of her offer, concluding with the immensely courteous and, under the circumstances, delightfully wry disclaimer that he knew all along she was not really serious, because "en la boca de las buenas señoras no ha de haber ninguna [habla] que sea mala" ("there can never be anything immoral in the mouths of good/virtuous/moral ladies").[20]

Here then is the Penguin translator's version of the colloquy between Sancho and the duchess:

> "Don't you worry, friend Sancho," said the duchess. "I will have my maids wash you, and scrub you if need be."
>
> "I'll be content if they do my beard," answered Sancho, "at least for the present; but for the rest Heaven will provide in due course."
>
> "Butler," said the duchess, "see what the good Sancho wants, and comply with his wishes in all respects."[21]

Where is the *gusto* (pleasure/delight) that Sancho has perceived, and the duchess has assured him he can have, if and when he wants it? Her maids "will scrub [him] if need be," which is neither what the Spanish says nor what either the lady or Sancho Panza has in mind. It may be sufficiently arousing for Mr. Cohen, but the duchess is neither so inexperienced nor so naive, and neither is Sancho. He declines but, obviously tempted, declines just barely, indicating that, "que andando el tiempo, Dios dijo lo que será" ("as time goes along/afterwards, God only knows what will happen"). Cohen has him say, blandly, "but for the rest Heaven will provide in due course." This is civil-servant rhetoric, as before, but neither the words nor the meaning square with the original. The butler is instructed to "comply with his wishes in all respects." There is no room for sly innuendo in such dull verbiage.

Messrs. Ormsby, Jones, and Douglas similarly bowdlerize:

> "Don't be uneasy, friend Sancho," said the duchess. "I will see that my ladies wash you, and even rinse and bleach you if necessary."
>
> "I'll be content with the beard," said Sancho, "at least for now; and as for the future, God knows."
>
> "Attend to worthy Sancho's request, steward," said the duchess, "and do exactly what he wishes."[22]

20. Vol. 2, chap. 44.
21. Trans. Cohen, 678–79.
22. Trans. OJD, 605.

Unless there is a risqué flavor to being rinsed and bleached, of which I am unaware, the sexuality has been scrubbed from this passage. Again, too, the *maestresala* (butler/steward) is told to "attend to worthy Sancho's request." How solemn our duchess has become! And how boring. (Who, by the way, ever said that Sancho was "uneasy"? He is nothing of the sort; rather, he is drolly interested, both inclined and disinclined, and plainly sorely tempted. The *words* of the Spanish may justify such a rendering, but the *meaning* absolutely does not.)

Starkie's translation squirms a bit more, in doing away with the vitality of the passage, but does the dirty deed nonetheless:

> "Do not worry, friend Sancho," said the duchess; "I will make my maids wash you, and even put you in the bath if necessary."
>
> "I'll be content with the beard," said Sancho, "at any rate for the present. As for the future, it's God's will what'll happen."
>
> "Carry out the worthy Sancho's request, seneschal," said the duchess, "and do exactly what he wishes."[23]

Starkie has so managed things, however, that if any sexual activity on Sancho's part is to result, the duchess's instructions to her "seneschal" would seem to indicate that he, and not the *doncellas,* is to engage in it. "Do exactly what he wishes," she commands. I need hardly say that this was not what Cervantes had in mind.

Nor does Smollett come off any better:

> "Give yourself no concern, friend Sancho, said the dutchess [*sic*], for, I will order my maids not only to wash, but also to lay you a bucking, should it be necessary." "I shall be satisfied with the lathering of my beard, replied the squire, at least for the present; and God will ordain what is to happen in the sequel." The dutchess turning to the major-domo, "Remember, said she, what honest Sancho desires, and gratify his inclination with the utmost punctuality."[24]

"To lay a bucking," a somewhat archaic expression, is not entirely clear; it may mean to "wash with lye," though that would truly be something about which Sancho might feel "uneasy." In any event, the colloquy is turned from lightly spiced to heavily squashed.

23. Trans. Starkie, 758.
24. Trans. Smollett, 607.

"Don't worry, friend Sancho," said the duchess, I'll make sure my young ladies wash you—and I'll even have them go further than that, if you like."

"Taking care of my beard will be good enough for me," answered Sancho, "at least for now—and later on, God knows what might happen."

"Butler," said the duchess, "pay attention to my good Sancho's request, and make sure he gets exactly what he wants."[25]

That is my own translation, and I'm afraid I can't help pointing out that this is both what the passage says and what it means. Note, too, that people speaking are here represented in speechlike terms. Cervantes knows the difference between expository and conversational prose, and so should his translator. I suspect that my readers will know not only that these are human beings speaking, but pretty exactly what kind of human beings. Nor do I think that Cervantes' charming characters will seem boring, dull, bureaucratic, or weary of the whole business.

Cervantes' handling of speech, indeed, is a major source of information for his readers. *How* the characters speak, as well as what they say, is extremely important. Don Quijote chatting with Sancho Panza, as they jog along, is stylistically a completely different affair than Don Quijote making a formal address to the duke or the duchess. And Cervantes is even more skillful, for Don Quijote by the end of the book does not speak quite the way Don Quijote did in the beginning. It is clear that he has learned from Sancho Panza—as Sancho Panza, too, has learned from Don Quijote. The colloquies between the two men shift in tone, subtly but palpably, across the long length of the novel. By the end, Don Quijote is quoting proverbs (Sancho's forte), and Sancho is sounding like the "retired" administrator he has (briefly) been. The literate man becomes more colloquial; the illiterate man becomes as good as lettered. It is marvelous writing—but how does one translate it?

As his master likes to complain, Sancho Panza's mouth is always open, his tongue always working. His words, quite as much as Don Quijote's, deeply, indelibly flavor the entire novel: getting them right, or as close to right as possible, is plainly crucial to any translation. Here is the very first thing Sancho ever says, the first time he in fact opens his mouth:

"Mire vuestra merced, señor caballero andante, que no se le olvide lo que de la ínsula me tiene prometido; que yo la sabré gobernar, por grande que sea."

25. Trans. Raffel.

Sancho's second speech, after a response from Don Quijote which is more than five times the length of his squire's comment, and is spoken in a very different tone and structured far more complexly,[26] is again in this same "downhome" style. And since both these speeches are very short, let me quote this second one as well:

> "De esa manera," respondió Sancho Panza, "si yo fuese rey por algún milagro de los que vuestra merced dice, por lo menos, Juana Gutiérrez, mi oíslo, vendría a ser reina, y mis hijos infantes."[27]

Neither of these speeches shows, or at this early point in the novel should show, Sancho in full conversational flight. Cervantes is far too subtle and masterful a writer to hurry either himself or his characters. What we are given, here, is an important but succinct introduction to several dominant themes and styles: (1) Sancho has become our knight's squire because he has been bribed, and he therefore takes Don Quijote's promises very seriously; as a nonliterate man, and—at this stage of the novel—someone who is not supposed to be overly bright, he wants explicit (and repeated) reassurance about those promises, and wants that reassurance in the only way meaningful to him, namely, orally; (2) Don Quijote may soar into elaborate historical (or pseudo-historical) flights, but Sancho's feet remain firmly on the ground; and (3) Sancho's rhetoric, at this stage of the novel, is elementary, basic in both lexicon and in its nonemployment of abstract or conceptual materials. Here are my versions of these two speeches:

> "Now be careful, your grace, sir knight errant, you don't forget that island you promised me, because no matter how big it is I'll know how to govern it."

> "So," said Sancho Panza, "if I become a king, by one of those miracles your grace is talking about, at the very least my old lady, Teresa, would get to be a queen, and my kids would be princes."[28]

Sancho is polite, by his peasant standards; he is respectful, again by his standards; but he is blunt, insistent, and obviously as out of touch

26. I will return to this speech by Don Quijote.

27. Vol. 1, chap. 7.

28. Sancho's wife is called by a number of names; since however "Teresa Panza" is the name on which Cervantes finally settled, and this is an authorial inconsistency rather than an issue of any substance, I have here normalized "Juana Gutiérrez"—which is what the Spanish text calls her, at this point—into "Teresa."

with reality, on some levels, as is his master. He is a mild braggart; he is also keenly aware both of his own low economic and social standing, and also of the fact that only through someone ranked higher than himself can he possibly raise his own standing. His rhetoric, as I have said, is colorfully folk-like, but culturally and socially limited, and it is important not to elevate it, just as it is important to present Sancho's speech as stylistically consistent: much of the character's "meaning" ("as opposed to mere lexical meaning") depends on the clarity of that presentation. And if, as we know he will, the character of Sancho is to develop and grow, and those later stages are to be accurately depicted, these initial representations must allow room for his development to be clear.

Here then are the same two speeches, as translated in the Penguin version:

> "Mind, your worship, good Sir Knight Errant, that you don't forget about the isle you promised me; for I shall know how to govern it, never mind how big it is."

> "At that rate," said Sancho Panza, "if by any of those miracles your worship speaks of I were to become king, Juana Gutierrez, my poppet, would be a queen, no less, and my children princes."[29]

Rhetoric rather than failure to track syntactical flow is the chief problem, here. (It would of course be hard to disturb syntactical flow in such short and straightforward material.) *Mire* ("consider/watch out/be careful") translated as "mind" rather jars on American ears, but it is standard British usage; the same is true of Cohen's rendering of the appellation "vuestra merced" ("your grace/worship"). British lawyers, for example, address the judge as "your worship" rather than "your honor," and there is in general a good deal more "worshipping" those of higher rank in the more class-conscious world of Britain than there is in the United States. But the second appellation Cervantes puts in Sancho's mouth is a plain, straightforward "señor caballero andante" ("sir knight errant"): to add "good" to that appellation, as Cohen does, suggests a formal elevation of diction false to Sancho's characterization. Spanish requires *que* ("that") in front of "no se le olvide" ("you don't forget"); English does not, and using "that" again incorrectly elevates the diction (and Sancho). Nor would Sancho, were he speaking modern English, use the poetic usage "isle"[30] for *ínsula* ("island"), rather than the straightforward "island." Sancho's

29. Trans. Cohen, 67.
30. See *The Penguin English Dictionary,* 389a, which clearly so labels the word "isle."

colloquial *que* ("because"), instead of the more formal *porque* ("because"), quite escapes Cohen, who turns this colloquial usage into the stiffly formal "for"—and this stiffness is still further emphasized by his rendering of "sabré gobernar" ("I'll know how to govern") as "I *shall* know how to govern." Both the auxiliary itself and its unspeechlike form ("I shall know" rather than "I'll know") present Sancho as someone he most definitely is not. Much the same thing happens when Cohen translates "de esa manera" ("in that way") as the highly formal "at that rate," a learned locution that Sancho simply would not use. The subjunctive *fuese* ("were") was and still is relatively common in Spanish, but in contemporary English even well-educated and literate people often go through their entire lives without ever using the subjunctive. To put it into Sancho's mouth is therefore a grave error. The Spanish "fuese rey" must be Englished "become *a* king"; "become king," as Cohen makes Sancho say (lazily? translating automatically, without thought?), means something quite different, namely, "to become *the* king." When a Spaniard speaks of "becoming king," absent any more explicit reference we are obliged to understand him as saying "become king *of Spain.*" Sancho is saying nothing of the sort. Translating *dice* ("says") as "speaks" is tonally false, as is "no less" for *por lo menos* ("at least"). Although "poppet" may be good colloquial usage in England, it cannot be used for "oíslo" (a slang word for "wife," when used by a man, and for "husband," when used by a woman), since in British usage it specifically refers to a small child, usually a little girl—not surprisingly, since its primary meaning was and to some extent still is "doll" or "marionette." To deprive *oíslo* of its marital context is, yet again, to bowdlerize—not consciously perhaps, but what does that matter?

Translating Cervantes' closely and carefully wrought textures and tones into such an ill-assorted mélange, how can a translator ever replicate the slow, subtle, and vitally important change in Sancho's speech? The answer, of course, is that he cannot: starting Sancho's spoken usage in such an unholy mixture of written and speech styles (and continuing him in such unsteady fashion, as Cohen does), no translator can hope to present a Sancho who comes close to matching Cervantes'. I cannot here trace out the entire process. But listen to Sancho almost at the end of the novel, reassuring his master that he, Don Quijote, has seen signs and omens where no such things are to be found:

> "He aquí, señor, rompidos y desbaratados estos agüeros, que no tienen que ver más con nuestros sucesos, según que yo imagino, aunque tonto, que con las nubes de antaño."[31]

31. Vol. 2, chap. 73.

> "Here you are, my lord: now these signs and omens of yours are
> smashed to pieces and all gone—and, anyway, it seems to me,
> fool though I may be, these things have no more to do with what
> happens to us than last year's clouds."[32]

Sancho has not become a bishop, or a university graduate. But can
anyone doubt that the level of his discourse has been very significantly raised? The reader may not consciously think of it, but the change
is (or should be) so marked that he or she cannot help, on some level,
becoming aware of it. Sancho's first speeches, juxtaposed against this
almost final one, tell one large part of the story of Cervantes' great
book.

> "Here, sir, are these omens broken and destroyed. They have
> nothing more to do with our fortunes, to my mind, than last
> year's clouds."[33]

Although this is only one sentence in a three-sentence speech, Cohen
manages to level it both in structure and in meaning. Sancho's way
of speech has acquired some of the sweep and lexicon of his betters,
but by breaking this not overly long sentence into two, Cohen deprives
it of any significant forward movement. Further, although Sancho is
careful to say "según que yo imagino, aunque tonto" ("according to how
it seems to me, though I'm a fool"), Cohen turns him into a crisply
authoritative admonisher of his master. "To my mind," Cohen translates,
dropping both the explicitly deferential tone and also any reference to
Sancho terming himself a fool. But Cervantes has not changed Sancho
that much: Cohen here raises an already elevated tone to totally inappropriate levels.

Something of the same sort—though, again, we cannot fully trace out a
process about which entire books have been written—happens, although
in reverse, to Don Quijote's speech. His long and delectable response to
Sancho's first-ever speech, mentioned above, runs like this:

> "Has de saber, amigo Sancho Panza, que fue costumbre muy
> usada de los caballeros andantes antiguos hacer gobernadores a
> sus escuderos de las ínsulas o reinos que ganaban, y yo tengo
> determinado de que por mí no falte tan agradecida usanza; antes
> pienso aventajarme en ella: porque ellos algunas veces, y quizás

32. Trans. Raffel.
33. Trans. Cohen, 931.

las más, esperaban a que sus escuderos fuesen viejos, y ya después
de hartos de servir y de llevar malos días y peores noches, les
daban algún titulo de conde, o, por lo mucho, de marqués, de
algún valle o provincia de poco más a menos; pero si tú vives y yo
vivo, bien podría ser que antes de seis días ganase yo tal reino,
que tuviese otros a él adherentes, que viniesen de molde para
coronarte por rey de uno dellos. Y no lo tengas a mucho: que
cosas y casos acontecen a los tales caballeros por modos tan
nunca vistos ni pensados, que con facilidad te podría dar aún más
de lo que te prometo."[34]

Verbally, at least, Don Quijote is here riding very high indeed. And the
steady, thoughtful sweep of his meditative, authoritative (not to say
magisterial) words is, as Cervantes intends, positively hypnotic. Oh, the
things I could tell you, he suggests, because for knights errant the world
throws up such unexpected and wonderful rewards, "por modos tan
nunca vistos ni pensados, que con facilidad te podría dar aún más de lo
que te prometo" ("by methods/ways/procedures so utterly unprece-
dented and even unthought of, that it might easily happen that I'll be able
to give you even more than I've promised you"). The Penguin translator is
of course more at home with such high and elevated pomposities, but for
all that he manages to destroy the steady, thoughtful march of Don
Quijote's words. This is accomplished by (a) turning Cervantes' two
sentences into four, and (b) permitting Don Quijote none of the quiet
grace that, early and late, marks virtually his every utterance. Cohen's Don
Quijote does not meditate; there is nothing dreamy about his speech, as
though his words are delighting and indeed hypnotizing himself, even
as they are having much the same effect on Sancho Panza. This is a Don
Quijote intent on the stark transmittal of information:

> "You must know, friend Sancho Panza, that it was a custom much
> in use among knights errant of old to make their squires gover-
> nors of the isles or kingdoms they won; and I am determined
> that, for my part, so beneficial a custom shall not lapse. On the
> contrary, I intend to improve on it: for they often, perhaps most
> often, waited till their squires were grown old; and when they
> were worn out in their service, from bad days and worse nights,
> they gave them some title of count, or perhaps marquis, of some
> valley or province of more or less importance. But if you live and
> I live, it may well be that before six days are gone by I may win

34. Vol. 1, chap. 7.

some kingdom with others depending on it, and one of them may prove just right for you to rule. Do not think this any great matter, for adventures befall knights errant in such unheard and unthought-of ways that I might easily be able to bestow on you even more than I promise."[35]

Don Quijote does not in fact pause, and then say "on the contrary." Instead of breaking the sentence with a period, thus setting up a black and white antinomy, Cervantes goes on, gracefully, "antes pienso" ("rather, I think/propose/plan . . . "). That graciousness is an important part of our knight's characterization; it needs to be transmitted at every point where Cervantes wants it to be transmitted. In his second sentence, too, Cohen falls into the dangerous trap of using "they" and "their" almost as they are used in the Spanish, with the result that pronoun references become distinctly confusing. But Don Quijote is a masterful rhetorician, throughout the novel. So too the Spanish says "les daban algún título de conde" ("gave them a title like count"), and once more Cohen mechanically apes the Spanish, turning this into the unidiomatic "They gave them some title of count." Again, Don Quijote does not ever speak this way—or this poorly. Our knight carefully fudges just what size of landed estate he may give his squire: "algún valle o provincia de poco más a menos" ("some valley or province, more or less"). But Cohen cobs this into "some valley or province of more or less importance," though it is size and not importance that is at issue, and the reason for Don Quijote's fudging is thus quite obscured. It is of course size, and therefore wealth, that Sancho is concerned with: the point is subtle but important. And what polished, smooth-talking aristocrat—a role in which Don Quijote casts himself—would ever say, clumsily, "Before six days are gone by"? "Otros a él adherentes" *can* mean, as Cohen translates it, "others depending on it." But it does not mean that, here; rather, it refers to subordinate realms that owe (and pay) allegiance to some larger kingdom. To "depend" can and does mean too many things to be usable in this context: again, Cohen either looks a word up in the dictionary and takes the first "meaning" he sees, or else knows only one meaning for a word and constantly uses it, regardless of context. No language works that way, Spanish least of all: as I have said, much of the strength and subtlcty of Spanish lie precisely in its almost oriental ability to shift, from one context to another, the sense to be drawn from particular words. Spanish of course comes by that oriental capacity very naturally, having been at least partially a Moorish kingdom (or kingdoms) for so many centuries.

35. Trans. Cohen, 67.

Accordingly, Don Quijote's speech, as I understand it, sounds like this:

> "You must know, Sancho Panza my friend, that it used to be very common, in ancient times, for knights errant to make their squires governor of whatever islands or regions they conquered, and I am resolved not to neglect this gracious custom—indeed, I intend to improve on it, for occasionally, and I suspect most of the time, they waited until their squires had grown old and fed up with such service, enduring bad days and even worse nights, and then gave them a title—count, or more often marquis of some valley or province, more or less. But if you and I both live, it could be that in less than a week[36] I'll have conquered a kingdom to which others pay allegiance, which would be just right for crowning you ruler of one of these subordinate domains. Nor should you think this in any way remarkable, for no one can possibly foresee or even imagine the way the world turns for such knights, so it could easily happen that I will be able to grant you still more than my promise."[37]

Toward the end of their final journey, however, when Don Quijote passionately advises Sancho Panza (who has no intention of whipping himself at all) not to whip himself so hard that he does serious damage, our knight's speech has become plainer and, having accommodated itself to Sancho's, also pithier and more worldly:

> "Mira, amigo, que no te hagas pedazos; da lugar que unos azotes aguarden a otros; no quieras apresurarte tanto en la carrera, que en la mitad della te falte el aliento; quiero decir que no te des tan recio, que te falte la vida antes de llegar al número deseado. Y porque no pierdas por carta de más ni de menos, yo estaré desde aparte, contando por este mi rosario los azotes que te dieres. Favorézcate el cielo conforme tu buena intención merece."[38]

The Penguin translation, to be sure, registers virtually none of these rhetorical changes: it remains in the same stilted key throughout:

36. Spanish counts days rather than weeks: *ocho días* (eight days) = "a week" and *quince días* (fifteen days) = "two weeks/a fortnight." Don Quijote says "seis días" ("six days"); I have tried to translate the concept rather than simply the words.

37. Trans. Raffel.

38. Vol. 2, chap. 71.

"Mind you do not cut yourself to pieces, friend. Let there be a pause between the strokes. Do not rush headlong forward and have your breath fail you in the middle. Do not lay it on so strong, I mean, that your life fails you before you reach the required number. And for fear you may lose by a card too many or too few, I will stand close by and count the lashes on this rosary of mine. May Heaven favour you as your good purpose deserves!"[39]

Don Quijote's four breathless instructions, unwound in one tumbling sentence, here have the breathlessness literally knocked out of them: perhaps for the imagined convenience of the determinedly middle-brow, modern reader, Cohen presents each instruction in a separate, flatly worded sentence of its own. I would like to think that even the modern reader is capable of appreciating Cervantes' prose more as Cervantes in fact wrote it:

"Be careful, my friend, not to cut yourself to pieces; take your time, stroke by stroke; don't rush and, halfway through, find you're out of breath; what I mean is, don't whip yourself so hard that, before you reach the required number, you leave this life behind. And so you keep an exact account, neither too much nor too little, I will stand over here and use my rosary beads to count the lashes you give yourself. May Heaven smile on you, as your good intentions deserve that it should."

But another example may make the point more clearly. When Don Quijote and Sancho visit the Spanish fleet, in Barcelona harbor, a great fuss is made and the commanding officer greets our knight by shaking his hand, embracing him, and declaring warmly:

"Este día señalaré yo con piedra blanca, por ser uno de los mejores que pienso llevar en mi vida, habiendo visto al señor don Quijote de la Mancha; tiempo y señal que nos muestra que en él se encierra y cifra todo el valor del andante caballería."[40]

The naval man's courteously flowery language has been consistently translated in literal terms. "Este día señalaré yo con piedra blanca" ("I will mark this day with a white stone") emerges, in most translations, as "This day . . . will I mark with a white stone,"[41] "I shall mark this day with

39. Trans. Cohen, 922.
40. Vol. 2, chap. 63.
41. Trans. Smollett, 791.

a white stone,"[42] "I shall mark today with a white stone,"[43] "I shall mark to-day with a white stone."[44] But though these would have been more or less adequate translations in the early seventeenth century, when most readers were thoroughly familiar with ancient Roman customs, in the late twentieth century no such knowledge can be assumed and no such translation is viable. As Luis Andrés Murillo notes, this is an expression "que aludía a la práctica romana de señalar, retóricamente, los días felices o aciagos" ("which alludes to the Roman practice of indicating/designating/ marking/signaling, rhetorically, happy or ominous/unfortunate/fatal days").[45] The very fact that so recent an editor, in a European edition, thinks it necessary to explain the matter, seems to me fairly conclusively to indicate that, in English-speaking cultures still less firmly grounded in the niceties of classical literature, we have no right to assume that readers will (in this special sense) know a white stone from a black one. Accordingly, Don Quijote having already been welcomed by an elaborate aural and visual show of naval courtesies, I have translated, here, "This will be a day for flying flags and banners." I am emphatically in the minority, thus translating, but I do not think I am in the wrong.

I should like to rest my case (and conclude this discussion) with the comparatively unremarkable paragraph that closes the nineteenth chapter of volume 2. There is to be a hugely expensive rural wedding, to the great pleasure of a rich man named Camacho (who does not really deserve but has won the lady to be married), and to the infinite and fatal sadness of a poor man named Basilio (who deserves but has lost the lady). The last sentence of the paragraph immediately preceding reads, in my translation, "Indeed, peace and happiness seemed to be leaping and frolicking all over the meadow."

> Otros muchos andaban ocupados en levantar andamios, de donde con comodidad pudiesen ver otra día las representaciones y danzas que se habían de hacer en aquel lugar dedicado para solenizar las bodas del rico Camacho y las exequias de Basilio. No quiso entrar en el lugar Don Quijote, aunque se lo pidieron así el labrador como el bachiller; pero él dio por disculpa, bastantísima a su parecer, ser costumbre de los caballeros andantes dormir por los campos y florestas antes que en los poblados, aunque fuese debajo de dorados techos; y con esto, se desvió un

42. Trans. OJD, 778.
43. Trans. Starkie, 981.
44. Trans. Cohen, 879.
45. Miguel de Cervantes Saavedra, *El Ingenioso Hidalgo Don Quijote de la Mancha,* ed. Luis Andrés Murillo (1978; Madrid: Clásicos Castalia, 1984), vol. 2, 107 n. 9.

> poco del camino, bien contra la voluntad de Sancho viniéndosele
> a la memoria el buen alojamiento que había tenido en el castillo
> o casa de don Diego.

I have termed this an unremarkable paragraph (but only in comparative
terms), for the writing is neither as explosive nor as brilliant as much to
be found in the novel. All the same, it seems to me an excellent test of the
translator, weaving together narrative and thematic strands in amazingly
deft language—unremarkable, indeed, as I have suggested, only in comparison to Cervantes himself, elsewhere in the book. It is rich, mellifluous
prose—and here is how other translators have handled it:

> Several other persons were engaged in erecting a platform from
> which people might conveniently see the plays and dances that
> were to be performed the next day on the spot dedicated to the
> celebration of the marriage of Camacho the rich and the obse-
> quies of Basilio. Don Quixote would not enter the village, for
> all the urgings of peasant and bachelor alike. He excused himself
> on the grounds, amply sufficient in his opinion, that knights-
> errant customarily slept in the fields and woods in preference to
> towns, even were it under gilded ceilings. So he turned aside a
> little from the road, very much against Sancho's will, as the good
> quarters he had enjoyed in the castle or house of Don Diego
> came back to his mind.[46]

Would it have been possible for Cervantes to write so ghastly a sentence
as the first one here? And—to focus on only two items—even though the
Spanish word order is "en el castillo o casa de don Diego" ("in the castle
or house of Don Diego"), can anyone doubt that Cervantes wants us to
understand that, though it is in fact simply a house, to Sancho, at this
moment, Don Diego's hospitable residence seems glowingly like a castle?
    Here is another version:

> Some others were briskly erecting platforms, from which people
> might more comfortably see the plays and dances that were to be
> performed the next day on the spot dedicated to the celebration
> of the marriage of the rich Camacho and the obsequies of Basilio.
> Don Quixote refused to enter the village, though the peasant and
> the bachelor urged him to do so, giving what he thought was a
> most valid excuse, that it was the custom of knights-errant to

46. Trans. OJD, 531.

sleep in the fields and woods in preference to populated places, even though it might be under gilded roofs, and so he turned aside from the road, much against Sancho's will, for he had still lingering memories of the good lodgings he had received in Don Diego's house or castle.[47]

Applying the same two standards, Starkie too has mangled the flowing prose of the first sentence and, though he has reversed the order of "house" and "castle," has not taken the trouble to make either word meaningful.

On to Tobias Smollett:

> A great many were employed in raising scaffolds, that they might view from them more commodiously the plays and dances which were to be in that place, to solemnize the nuptials of Camacho the rich, and the obsequies of Basilius. Don Quixote refused to enter the village, tho' both the batchelor and the countryman invited him; but he pleaded what he thought a sufficient excuse, the custom of knights-errant to sleep in fields and forests, rather than in towns, tho' under gilded roofs; and therefore he turned a little aside, grievously against the will of Sancho, who had not yet forgotten the good lodgings he had enjoyed at the house of Don Diego.[48]

Smollett has caught much of the swing and lilt of the first sentence; even his somewhat dated language cannot disguise the freshness of the writing here. But on the second test Smollett fails, for the only way he seems to have seen open to him was to eliminate the "house/castle" comparison. His version makes good sense—better sense, clearly, than any of the versions thus far—but is it Cervantes' sense?

Here then is the Penguin translation:

> There were many others busily raising platforms, from which next day they would be able to see in comfort the plays and dances which were to be performed in that spot, dedicated to the celebration of the rich Camacho's wedding and Basilio's funeral. Don Quixote refused to enter the village, although both the peasant and the student begged him to, giving what seemed to him a most sufficient excuse: that it was the custom of knights

47. Trans. Starkie, 663.
48. Trans. Smollett, 533.

errant to sleep in the fields and woods rather than in towns or villages, even though it were under gilded roofs. Therefore he went a little way off the road, much against Sancho's will, for the good lodging he had had in Don Diego's castle or house was still fresh in the squire's memory.[49]

In capturing the style of the first sentence, Cohen does somewhat better than some, but not nearly so well as Smollett. This is not ghastly prose, and that is of course the Penguin standard: "not ghastly" = "acceptable." Can Cervantes be thus translated? That is, when you translate by such a standard, can you hope to come up with a translation that in any true sense of the word *is* Cervantes' book? Cohen's handling of the second item, the "house/castle" comparison, is manifestly as bad as any.

Finally, here is my own translation:

> There were a good many people putting up scaffolding, from which, the next day, they would be better able to watch all the dancing and the performances scheduled to take place, in honor of the rich Camacho's wedding and poor Basilio's funeral. Don Quijote would not enter the village, though both the peasants and the university students begged him to, but excused himself (more than sufficiently, to his way of thinking) by explaining that knights errant customarily slept in the fields and forests, rather than in populated places and under gilded roofs. So he rode a little way off the road (much against Sancho's better judgment, who could not help remembering how well he'd been accommodated in Don Diego's house—or castle, as it seemed to him.)

To apply the test of tracking syntactic flow: the Spanish spreads through two very long sentences, clause after rolling clause. My translation uses three sentences, broken by 10 commas and a pair of parentheses; OJD, 4 sentences and 5 commas; Starkie, 2 sentences and 8 commas; Smollett, 2 sentences, 8 commas, and 2 semicolons; and Cohen, 3 sentences, 7 commas, and 1 colon. This test alone is sufficient to disqualify OJD; it is not sufficient to fully evaluate the other translations. Lexical and other sorts of examinations demonstrate, however, that although Smollett well matches the original in some respects, in others he fails. I would argue that only my own version passes tests on all the

49. Trans. Cohen, 593-94.

assorted levels. Though no one can or in my opinion ever will match Cervantes' magnificent prose, I think that all in all I have come the closest, to date, of anyone who has tried to English the greatest novel ever written. And, as I said, on that I rest my case and close my book.

Appendix

Procedures Used in Selecting Sample Texts

Since I fully accept (and myself teach) linguistics as a science, even as I insist that in certain of its domains linguistics (like such related disciplines as anthropology) necessarily both borders on and even becomes in part an art, I approached Part 1 of this book very much as, almost fifty years ago, I approached the laboratory problems in first-year physics, which was at that time meant to be my major field of study. Accordingly, the decision to confine Chapter 1, "The Linguistics of Prose Versus the Linguistics of Verse," to translations *from* English was completely conditioned, as the first sentence of that chapter suggests, by the fact that my primary concern, both as a translator and as a commentator on translation, is with translation *into* English. That is, if my remarks about the differing natures of prose and verse were to apply to, and be valid in, the subsequent discussion of translation *into* English, they also had to be valid—linguistics being as I have said for the most part a science—when applied to translation *from* English. A physics experiment that recognizes that the momentum-energy of moving object A affects the inertia-energy of standing object B must also account for the inertia of object B simultaneously affecting the momentum-energy of object A. And since it is for me a working principle that, no matter what other people may be capable of, I must limit myself to translation into English—and must never write for publication in any language but English—I took advantage, in this first chapter, of the fact that Old English, prose and poetry alike, today requires translation to be understood by readers of Modern English. It seemed to me, further, that if I postponed, for the moment, discussion of translation *into* English, I might more objectively establish guidelines for Part 1's central pages, which deal exclusively with such translation.

As in Chapter 2 I moved to discussion of translation *from* other languages and *into* English, the same laboratory-style approach dictated that I begin with a language as utterly unlike English and its associated Indo-European tongues as I could manage. Taking the first non-English text from Indonesian, an Austro-Polynesian language with a totally different phonology, morphology, and syntax, as well as with a lexicon almost one hundred percent distinct from that of English, offered exactly the high contrast I needed and wanted. Not a great deal of Indonesian prose has been translated into English, and since I wanted a literary sample, and twenty-odd years ago, in my first book on translation, *The Forked Tongue,* had put into print three different versions of a passage from Achdiat K. Mihardja's 1949 novel, *Atheis (The Atheist),* and a fourth and complete translation of this novel had subsequently been published, it seemed the logical choice.

I frankly expected, once I had established reasonably specific guidelines for prose translation from Indonesian, that I would find quite different guidelines when I then turned to prose translation from the assorted Indo-European languages that are, for good historical reasons, the principal source tongues for prose translation into English. Let me be more specific: with the exception of the general importance of syntax for prose translation, a fact of which I became sharply cognizant when I translated first Rabelais's *Gargantua and Pantagruel* and then Cervantes' *Don Quijote* (the first substantial prose texts I had ever translated), I had not in fact formulated guidelines, either for prose translation from Indonesian into English or for prose translation from any other tongue. And, truthfully, I was at that point operating on the working hypothesis, which seemed to me a sound one, that though syntax might well be important across-the-board, the striking differences among the syntactic procedures of *all* human languages would necessarily be reflected (I was not yet sure just how) in the guidelines that could be developed for each individual language. Once again, this was an experimental process much like that followed in physics and in the other so-called hard sciences: having developed an apparently sound working model, one tests that model in operation, compares actual results with predicted results, and makes whatever changes may be needed in the model. An infinity of such experiments would of course be required to arrive, finally, at an absolute operating theory—which would then be entitled to be termed an explanation rather than a mere theory. But in real life, to be sure, one cannot perform an infinity of experiments, and a reasonable number is considered sufficient—unless and until another experimenter performs the same or a closely similar experiment with a new language and obtains new and differing results, at which point the theory must of course be revised to take those results into account.

What I found, unexpectedly, was that syntax is even more important to the translation of prose than I had thought. Syntax does indeed differ from language to language, and no one can reproduce the syntax of any language in any other language. But apparently because the movement, the flow, of prose syntax so closely represents the movement of the writer's mind, a general approximation, or "tracking," of that syntactic flow was not only possible, in translating prose into English, even from so very different a language as Indonesian, but was in fact required. I had not been consciously aware of any such considerations when almost thirty years earlier I made my contribution to the translation of the novel *Atheis,* but all the same my working procedures seemed to have been consistent with this quite unexpected finding.

This of course changed, and necessarily changed, some of the way in which I proceeded to choose further examples for analysis: it became necessary, now, to test my unexpected finding as harshly as I could, to see if indeed it would hold up. I chose French and then German, as Indo-European tongues very distinct both from English and from Indonesian, and I started with a literary text of approximately equivalent French prose from a Guy de Maupassant story. (By "approximately equivalent" I mean having no great disparity in literary approach.) I did not want, at this point, to introduce questions of chronology, as I might later need to do, if the unexpected finding began to assume more universal theoretical standing. The literary chronology of Indonesia being objectively shorter than that of France (that is, literature in the Indonesian language having begun much, much later), but Indonesian literature having moved through its various phases much more quickly, in chronologically compressed fashion, de Maupassant seemed about as good a counterpart to Mihardja as one could find. Nor did I, again at this point, want to complicate matters with nonfictional prose, as once again I might need to do (and in the event did) at some later point.

Finding that the tracking of syntactic flow was in truth an important guideline for the translation into English of French prose, as well as the translation into English of Indonesian prose, and in much the same manner, I carefully chose my next sample from yet another Indo-European tongue, German, once more a language (not to mention a literary tradition) distinctly unlike English, Indonesian, or French. I also decided to perhaps tempt fate a bit, by introducing some chronological differences—nothing terribly drastic, but enough to discover, perhaps, if chronology might be likely to affect the results. Working with translations of a passage from Heinrich Heine's early-nineteenth-century *Die Harzreise,* accordingly, I yet again found syntactic tracking to be an important and reliable guide.

At this point it seemed important to me, as I began Chapter 3, that I expand the horizons of my sample passages and, in a series of experiments, gradually introduce a variety of complexities and complications. Translation of literary prose being the principal issue, and there being no more basic text of literary prose than Gustave Flaubert's *Madame Bovary,* I opened Chapter 3 with a discussion of six very different translations of that novel into English, made at a variety of times and by translators from a variety of backgrounds. As expected, this procedure produced complexities in the formulation of the theory, notably that tracking syntactic flow is a *sine qua non* but not a guarantee for effective prose translation; lexical issues play the next most important role, followed by assorted other stylistic matters. It being appropriate, this having been determined, to next introduce chronological considerations, I chose Boccaccio's famous fourteenth-century prose text, the *Decameron,* a choice that also allowed me to work with yet another Indo-European tongue. When this analysis too produced no significant change in the now well-developing theory, I switched at the start of Chapter 4 to still another Indo-European tongue, Spanish. And when the theory survived that analysis essentially intact, I decided not only to choose a text that invoked truly large chronological issues, but also one (a) that involved a completely different Indo-European tongue, Latin, and (b) a text that, although clearly literary, was not fiction but autobiography, namely, Saint Augustine's *Confessions.* That analysis having satisfied me that, in essence, the theory was going to be valid pretty much wherever I looked (at least, given my own linguistic limitations), I allowed myself the comparative luxury of returning to French, my own primary foreign tongue, and also a language in which multiple translations of classic prose literary texts would be readily available. (Availability of multiple translations is of course yet another *sine qua non* for this entire discussion, much like the analyst's linguistic capacities: I would have liked to consider such languages as Chinese and Japanese, and Swahili, and more, but I do not command those tongues.) Accordingly, I completed Chapter 4, and the book's more theoretical first part, with two novels by Balzac, one by Zola, and, finally, with a discussion of translating Marcel Proust's great novel (the only possible rival to

Madame Bovary, if one wants to choose a single most important work of French literary prose), *À la recherche du temps perdu.*

Part 2 of the book concerns two classic translations I have myself recently made, and, its approach being rather more practice- than theory-oriented, no element of language-choice was there relevant.

Index

Consecutive page numbers in *italics* refer to the primary discussion.